Lectora® 201: What They *Don't* Tell You In Class

Classes are great.

Coaching is great.

And experience is the best teacher – **but it's expensive!**

There is a lot to be learned about using any piece of software, a lot more than they have time to teach you in a class. And even if they did, you probably wouldn't retain it. So, I have collected a lot of the experience of others and pulled it together here in one place. It contains:

172 Tips to help you get your work done faster and get on with the important things in life

32 Differences between what you see and how things behave in Lectora Run mode and HTML.

57 Warnings to keep you help you learn from other's mistakes

Books by the Author

Effective eLearning Design series:

Vol. 1: Designing Effective eLearning: A Step-by-Step Guide

Vol. 2: Superb eLearning using Low-Cost Scenarios: A Step-by-Step Guide to eLearning by Doing

Vol. 3: ILT to CBT (hopefully 2015)

Mastering Lectora® series:

Lectora 101: Ten Easy Steps for Beginners

Lectora 201: What They Don't Tell You in Class

Lectora 301: Techniques for Professionals

About the Author

Ben Pitman is a training and instructional design professional with over 20 years of experience. He is a Certified Internet Webmaster and holds a Ph.D. in Human Resource Development majoring in adult learning. He has been developing training for over 20 years and e-learning courses for over 10 years. He has helped thousands of people with Lectora problems on the community forum and is known there as "Dr. Lectora."

Ben would be glad to help you with designing e-learning as well as development in Lectora. Here is his contact information:

ben.pitman@eProficiency.com
678-571-4179 in Atlanta, GA
www.eProficiency.com

Lectora® 201:

What They *Don't* Tell You in Class

Edition 2.0
October 2014

Benjamin Pitman, Ph.D.
a.k.a. Dr. Lectora

iv

© Copyright 2014, Benjamin Pitman, Suwanee, GA, USA

eProficiency, Inc.
1810 Chattahoochee Run Drive
Suwanee, GA 30024
678-571-4179
www.eProficiency.com

For general information on other products and services including training and coaching, or technical support, please visit www.eProficiency.com or contact Ben Pitman at 678-571-4179, support@eProficiency.com.

Trademarks: Windows®, Microsoft®, Microsoft® MS Word, and PowerPoint®® are registered trademarks of Microsoft® Corporation. Lectora® is a registered trademark of Trivantis Corporation. Flash® is a registered trademark of Adobe Systems Inc. Other product and company names mentioned herein may be the trademarks of their respective owners. Use of trademarks or product names is not intended to convey endorsement or affiliation with this book.

Library of Congress Cataloging-in-Publication Data

Pitman, Benjamin.

Lectora 201: What They Don't Tell You In Class

Includes index.

ISBN-13: 978-1499215052

ISBN-10: 1499215053

1. Lectora. 2. Computer-based training development. 3. Authoring tools. 4. Authoring Applications. 5. Web-based training development.

To my brothers, Chris and Mark,
and their wives Julia and Nancy

And of course, to my wife who always shed light on those dark days.

Contents

Introduction

My focus for this book is on you developing courses in less time with less frustration. What you have here is years of experience boiled down into a single reference source. If you choose to master its contents, you will save yourself a lot of grief and amaze your co-workers.

My focus is not on perfect grammar or beautiful graphics. Personally, I get bored with formal third-person documents that explain how to do things. I intentionally, I wrote it as if I were talking directly to you. Here and there, I took a few liberties with the English language (no fainting). Mainly, rather than put "he/she" or default to "he" or swap arbitrarily back and forth between "he" and "she," I used "they" in many cases. Once in a while you may find incomplete sentences like you would use when you are talking to someone. Just remember my intent – to help you to write better e-learning courses.

I write using a lot of bullets and tables. I am not one for long wordy explanations or summarizing research.

This is a companion book to my other Lectora books, *Lectora 101* and *Lectora 301*.

Goal of This Book

All applications have their quirks and limitations. Lectora is no different. Being aware of them and knowing how to work around them will save you tons of time and effort as well as reducing your frustration level.

In this book, you will find tips, tricks, techniques, and workarounds for speeding up Lectora development. I have learned either from working with Lectora or from the Lectora Community Forum. I don't claim to have invented all of these but I have compiled them into one place where you can find them as a handy resource.

But, Is This Book for You?

The answer is "yes" if you:

- Want to develop better courses faster in Lectora
- Avoid the mistakes others have made
- Are willing to read a little each day and apply the tips, and
- Have completed Lectora basic training and have been using Lectora regularly for a month or so.

Warning: If you do not want to do things faster, are not willing to work at it, or do not have the proper Lectora experience, then this book is probably a waste of your time and money. You will probably not appreciate many of the tips, understand them, or remember them.

Symbols and Terms

Warning: This indicates an area you should exercise caution.

All warnings are summarized in Appendix 1.

And just to be clear, here is how I use a few of the more common words that appear in e-learning literature.

Term	How I Used It
Course	Lesson, module, or Lectora title – I make no distinction between these in this book.
Design	I use "design" to refer to the entire process of figuring out what you are going to present and how you will do it. This covers creating an outline through building a storyboard.
Development	I use "develop" to refer to the process of taking the storyboard and moving it into an authoring tool that will present the content online.

Don't Try to Read This Book All at Once.

Do not sit down and read this book from cover to cover. You will drown in information and you won't remember much. Instead, look over the table of contents. Then flip through the book to get an idea what is in it and how it is organized.

Now you have an idea of what the book is really about. Do two things.

- Set aside 10 minutes a day to get better at Lectora. When you get to the office or start to work at your desk at home, commit to reading a couple of pages. Then try to apply them during the day.
- Whenever something does not look or work the way you think it should, don't spend hours trying to get it right and think you are a dummy. Instead, see if there is something about it in this book.

Where to Look

Finding a way to group all these tips was a real challenge. Here is where I ended up.

If you are looking for	Look in this chapter
Broad strokes to increase your productivity including tips on software configuration and even using storyboards	1. General Tips for Faster Development
Tips on how to work more effectively with the different objects in Lectora	2. Power Tips for Specific Objects
Ways to speed up getting your course reviewed, making corrections, publishing, and testing your course to be sure it works correctly	3. Reviewing, Publishing, and Testing Tips
Even more things to look out for when you are publishing to some form of HTML	4. Look Out for Lectora-HTML Differences
How to use the translation tool safely **even if you are not translating** (yes, it is a powerful tool for other things)	5. Tips for Using the Translations Tool
The big things to avoid because things either done look like they should or work like you expect	Appendix 1: Summary of Warnings

Well, let's get started!

1. General Tips for Faster Development

"Speed is not always the answer, but it sure can help at times."

Unknown

This book is devoted to you being able to do your job faster and learn from other people's mistakes. There are many things you can do each will help you – some more, some less. Some of it is getting the right **tools** to do the job. Some of it is using the right **techniques.** Sometimes starting at the bottom and working up is a lot faster than working from the top down. Skim through them, then implement one or two a day.

This section describes how to create a better development environment. It gives you tips on how to configure your computer and a variety of tools and techniques to make life easier.

A. Get the Right Hardware and Software Configuration

Having the right hardware and the right software settings can go a long way to speeding up your work. This section gives you tips on some of the cheapest and easiest things you can do to increase your productivity by adding just a bit of hardware and making some minor adjustments to how your system is configured. These have little or nothing to do with Lectora itself, which may be a reason you didn't learn about them in class. They just make it easier to use.

Tip 1: How to Get More Out of the System You Have

I have seen people try to develop courses in Lectora with screens not much bigger than their course window size. They have to reduce the size of the layout area, which leads to inaccurate layouts, or they are constantly scrolling around.

Make the resolution of your monitor as high as possible and still be readable. It's like having a bigger desk. At first, you may find the small type size strange, but give it 5-10 minutes. Then decide. The more space you have on your screen to work with, the more you can spread out and not have to spend all your time flipping through open Windows®.

For Windows® XP right click on your desktop and select Properties. For Vista and Windows® 7, and 8 find the Display Properties. Click on the Settings tab and try the various settings under Screen resolution as shown below. You will have to click the Apply button to see the difference. Select the largest one you read that works with your monitor.

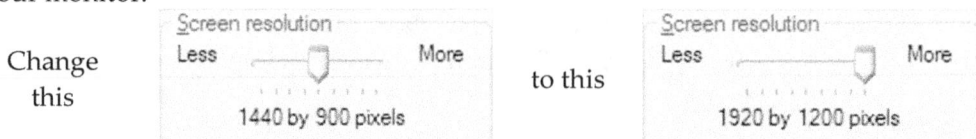

Tip 2: The Cheapest Way to *Increase* Your Productivity

Use two monitors instead of one. It gives you a lot more real estate to work with. You can put the storyboard or your graphic art tool on one and your Lectora title on the other. It is a *lot* faster to copy and paste things from one document to another when you can see them both at the same time. Make sure both your monitors have high resolution, 1600 or better.

Tip 3: Get a Low Cost Tool for Creating Compact Images

One of the greatest inventions since sliced bread – SnagIt. Use it for all kinds of stuff. If you just copy and paste from PowerPoint® and some other drawing tools, you can end up with huge file sizes for your images. Just pasting a picture results in a bit map image and could easily take 200-300k. These are compressed when you publish but they still take a lot of space, especially for bigger courses.

When PowerPoint® drawings don't paste well into Lectora, this is a great cheap tool. What works wonders is to set up a **profile** in SnagIt to capture from the Clipboard and save to a file. Here's how this technique works.

- Set up some kind of automatic naming in the SnagIt profile and have them always saved to a folder. I call mine SnagIt Files and put it on my desktop.

- I set the Resolution in the profile to 96 dpi. This is the default dpi for Windows® machines and seems to work fine for Macs, which use 72.

- Add any other things to the profile you want like a border or shadow. I generally do these in the drawing tool so they are consistent

- Open the SnagIt output folder beside Lectora. Then the process looks like this to get the graphic into Lectora with SnagIt open in the background.
    - In PowerPoint®, copy the desired boxes & lines.

    - Press the SnagIt hot key combination (I like Ctrl+Shift+C) to convert the object to a JPG and put in the output folder. (This puts the image at bottom of the list in the SnagIt folder so I know exactly where to look for it.)

    - Drag and drop the image from the SnagIt folder onto the Lectora page.

Use SnagIt for lots of other graphics stuff like adding shadows and adding a glow all around an image. It is not perfect and yes, there are better tools, but it is cheap and easy to learn – a big plus.

Note: As of today, Feb 28, 2014, SnagIt cannot yet create PNGs *with* transparency as part of the profile. When I need that, I use FireWorks but any drawing tool that supports transparent PNGs will work. Use PNG32.

Tip 4: How to Speed up the Font Drop-Down List

When you click on the font list, it may take a bit for the list to appear because it is being formatted with all the different fonts. If you find there are many fonts you never use, you can create a second folder in your C:\Windows® folder and move the fonts you don't use from the Fonts folder to it. Now the font dropdown list will appear more quickly and it makes it easier to find the fonts you do want.

Tip 5: Use the Right Windows® Settings for Development

Warning 1: Using any Display setting in Windows® other than 100% can result in faulty page layout.

When you are using Lectora, be sure to have the correct Display settings in Windows® 8 and probably 7. Here is a text box with seven words on the first line. I used SnagIt to grab the box. I had the Windows® Display size set to Smaller – 100%.

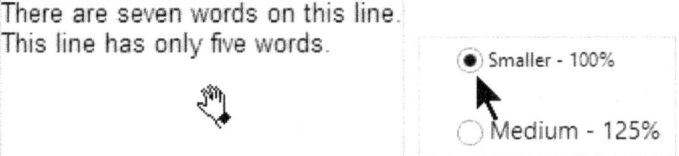

Now, here is the same text box captured the same way with the Display size set to Medium – 125%. Now it only has five words showing and is a bit smaller. This can seriously affect how you layout a page!

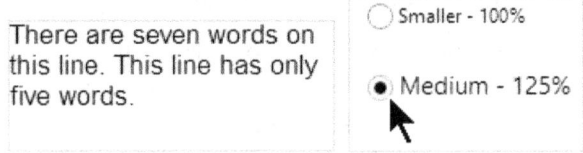

These settings are found in the Display area of the Control Panel.

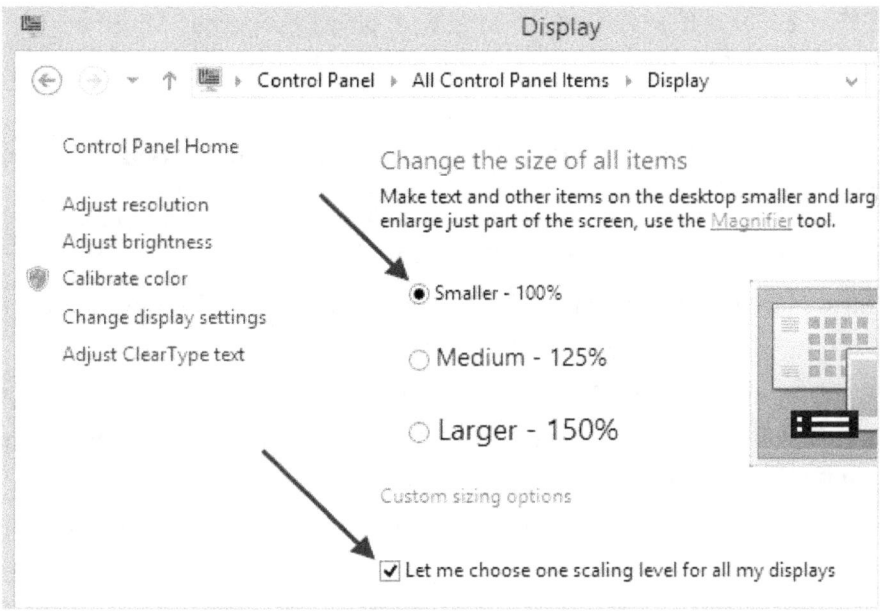

Tip 6: Opening the Course Twice

Sometimes I find it helpful to have two Windows open to the course so I can copy stuff from one place and paste into another. I just have to be careful which one I am making the changes in.

Warning 2: Unlike MS Word where both copies reflect changes made in either one, **Lectora copies are independent**. If you make changes to the first and save and close it then make changes to the second and save it, the changes to the first are GONE!

If you need to see one part of the course while working on another, here are some workarounds.

- Use Preview in Browser on one page and work on the other in Lectora.

- Publish it and view the published version.

- Copy the AWT file and open it. To keep your head straight, I have found that if I add a big "C O P Y" graphic to the background it helps me remember which is the copy.

B. Make Life Easier with These Across-the-Board Lectora Tips

These tips cover a wide range of ways you can speed things up when using Lectora. They did not fall under any of the other groups as many seemed to apply across-the-board. They cover better ways of working with object properties, shortcuts for doing things, and safe ways to do things so you don't get burned.

Tip 7: A Quick Way to Change Common Properties

One of the nice new things with Lectora 11 is that you can select a number of objects and change the *common properties* of all of them at the same time.

- For text objects, you can change all the font characteristics, background color, border, outline, and margin at one time.
- For several Lectora shapes, you can change the color, border, etc. at one time.
- For a mixed set of objects, you can only change the properties that they have in common like Initially Hidden or Always On Top.

All you have to do is select all the desired objects and then change the desired properties.

Tip 8: Get the Properties Ribbon Active Quickly

There are a number of ways to get to the Properties ribbon. The fastest is to simply:

- Double click on the object icon in the Title Explorer or
- Double click on any object in the layout pane except a text block

Tip 9: Save Yourself Time and Grief Using a Circus Approach

On one project I was working on, the Captivate developer spent several weeks creating 30 annotated movies and then handed them off to me. I inserted them only to find that the font sizes they used were too big and that the On Done Playing action we were depending on did not work. A better approach would have been to capture *one* movie and annotate. Insert into Lectora, publish to HTML, and get it reviewed by stakeholders before building the rest.

P.T. Barnum of circus fame used to say, "**Try it out in the small towns before taking it to the big city.**" Take the same approach with your development.

1. **New Courses:** Create a prototype of your course with sample pages, especially questions/exercises, and run it by your requestor and a target learner before developing 50 pages and have to redo them. Get them to approve the appearance and how the pages behave, especially the questions, the first time through *as well as how they behave when* the learner **returns** to the page later.

2. **New Stuff in Existing Courses:** Any time you are using a new approach or technique in a course, try it out in the target publish mode before creating many like it. Here are some examples:

   – If you are going to limit the learner to two tries on a Test question, get your actions to work on just one question before coding them on 10 questions.

   – If you want to do something special on the Test Results page based on the Test score, start with just 2 or 3 questions rather than 10-20.

   – If you are using audio with things being shown at the time they are being talked about in the audio, do it with one audio file and make sure it works when published and from your server.

Tip 10: The Safest Way to Open Your Course

Warning 3: You can accidently open the wrong course if you launch Lectora first.

While things have gotten better over the years, I still recommend opening a course by navigating to the folder in Windows® first and then double clicking on the course.

Over the years working with many clients and teaching courses, I have seen too many people open Lectora first and then open the desired course. Later, they could not find their course because they had lost track of it in Windows®.

Opening it by opening Lectora first can lead to confusion as to exactly where the course is. If you ever need to go into any of the folders like images, external, or media, or need to get an export from Lectora like a translate file, MS Word file, or zip file, you will know for sure where it is and that folder is already open.

Tip 11: Best Practice for Creating a Copy of a Course

Warning 4: Be absolutely sure you know what you are doing and which folder you are in when using Save As.

One person I worked with actually ended up with *nine* different versions of the course because he kept saving it to the wrong place.

Instead, in Windows®, copy the entire folder. Then go into the folder and change the name and open it by double clicking. I strongly recommend you avoid Save As.

Tip 12: Where Your Course Should Live

Warning 5: You can have problems if you open a course that is somewhere other than on your C drive. Not always, but when it does happen, the errors and problems do not indicate that the problem is related to where the course is stored.

The folders where your courses live when you are working on them should be on your C drive, *not* on the LAN or some server. Yes, it might work for a while, but then I have seen as well as heard of Lectora blowing off, losing images, and not publishing. If your company wants it on the LAN, copy the folder to your C drive, work on it there, and copy that folder back to the LAN twice a day.

Tip 13: Protect Yourself

This won't hurt anything or slow you down. On the file menu, go to the Save Options tab. There Check Enable Auto Save and set it to do that every minute.

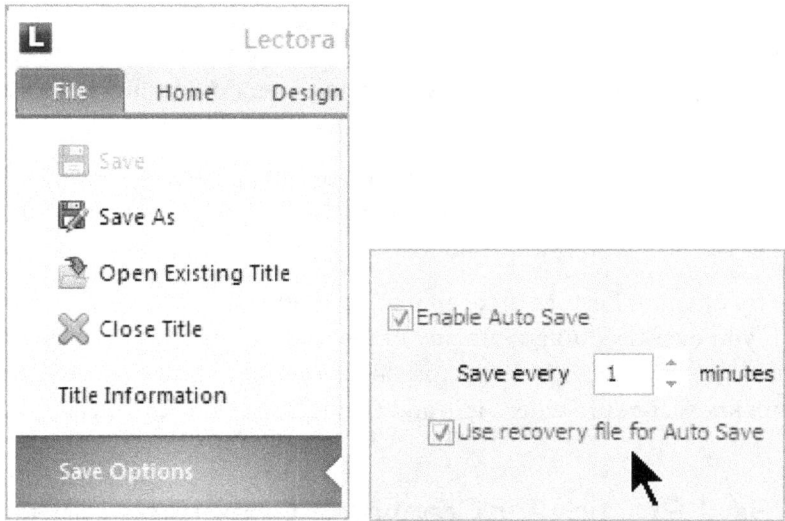

Tip 14: Secrets to Printable Page Sizes

If you are planning to have the learner be able to print Lectora pages, here are some specs that may interest you. This was before all the fancy scaling of the new browsers. If you think people may print the pages, try them to be sure they look the way you want them to.

Printing portrait mode: 672 x 872 is about the printable area for a portrait page Landscape page: 910 x 670. Remember you have to have the learner change the printer orientation because you cannot do this from within an HTML page (at least not very easily w/o Flash or some very fancy IE CSS styles. IE7 and onward seem to have some options for compressing the printable page.)

Tip 15: Printing in Landscape Mode

Most screens are landscape but when the learner goes to print, the right side of the page is frequently truncated because the printer is printing in portrait mode. One workaround is to provide a Print button and then display a warning message that the user needs to change to Landscape mode. You can use a variable to display this message only once. Some settings in IE7 and beyond will scale the output to fit on the page. If you don't see a menu bar like below, press the Alt key or right click in a blank area at the top of the browser and select Menu Bar.

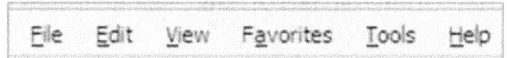

Then check Enable Shrink-to-Fit.

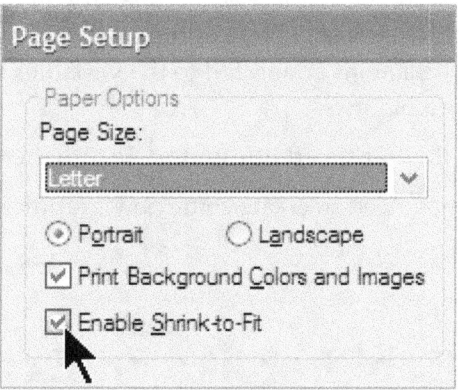

Be sure to try it out to be sure you can still read the page when printed.

Tip 16: Easily Make the Course More Interesting with Random Numbers

One way to make courses more interesting is to allow the learner to repeat a section but change the activities (accomplish this using questions). Have several questions on a page, all hidden. Use the Random function to select one of three questions (RAND(1,3)) by assigning a random number to a variable (Ex. _selection). Then have actions that show one of three questions with conditions based on the random number in the variable. (Ex. VAR(_selection) in the Condition Value field.)

"To select a random number, enter RAND(min, max) in the Value field. The random number assigned will be greater than or equal to the min value specified and less than or equal to the max value specified. The random number generated will be used to modify the Target variable." (Lectora Online Help)

Tip 17: Expert Recommendations If You Have Two Versions of the Course in One Lectora Title

Sometimes you may have two versions of a course in a single title – one English, one Spanish, one for Eastern Region employees, one for Western. After having done several of these, I personally recommend that you copy the course and have two separate versions on the LMS.

If your boss/client insists on both versions in the same title, then these tips are for you.

1. Create the title for one version.

2. Copy the AWT file.

3. Make the changes to it for the second version like translate it or change things for a different region.

4. Change the name of all the variables that are unique to the translated version like question numbers. Do something like add "_spa" if you were doing a translation to Spanish. Why? Because when, in a later step, you copy these pages back into the English title, all the actions connected to the variables will remain intact. Otherwise, you will have a big mess.

5. Copy all chapters in the translated title and paste into the original title.

6. If you need to, you may need to create some new graphics with translated words on them.

C. Use the Title Explorer like an Expert

Knowing how to use the Title Explorer is key to you being effective using Lectora. Here are a bunch of tips how to make it more friendly, readable, and even one on how to copy and paste *without* using the keyboard or the Lectora Library.

Tip 18: Use This Tool to Make the Title Explorer More Friendly

Again, in File ribbon > Preferences check the box to "Show buttons for hiding objects in the Title Explorer." This has no effect on what you see in the layout pane.

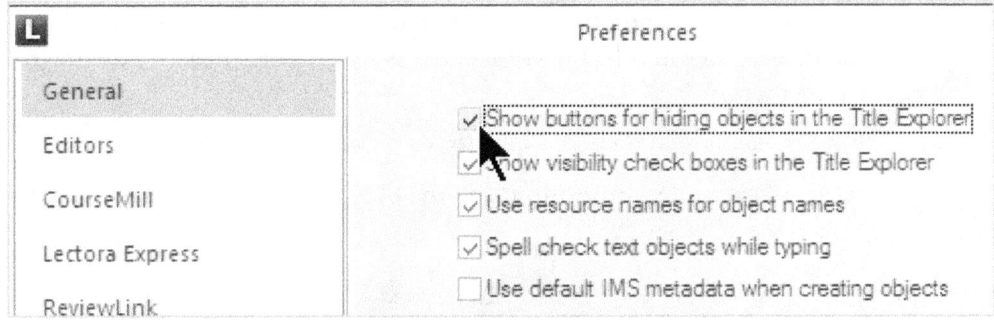

It shows a kind of hard to see box next to objects that are inherited at the title, AU, chapter, or section level. Below on the left you see all the chapter level objects. They can occupy a lot of space. On the right you see them all collapsed to a single line showing *"hidden objects."*

Before:

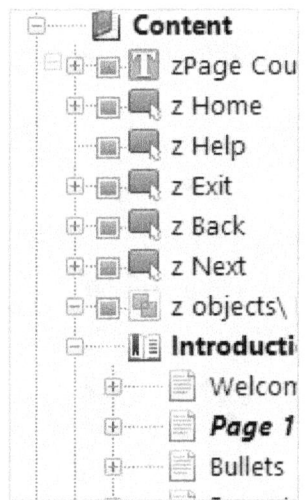

After clicking the box:

Tip 19: Another Tool to Make the Title Explorer More Readable

Organize objects that go together into groups. Once you do, you can move the group all at once, as if you do in PowerPoint® *and* you can hide the whole thing with one click or one action.

Here's how to group objects:

NOTE: objects to be grouped must all be at the same level (in the same page, section, chapter, or all at the title level).

1. Select your objects to be grouped by either selecting them in the Title Explorer or in the layout pane. You can select multiple objects by holding the Ctrl key down and clicking on them.

2. Right click your selection and choose Group from the popup menu.

You can collapse and expand your group using the plus (+) and minus (-) icon next to the group name.

Expanded   Collapsed

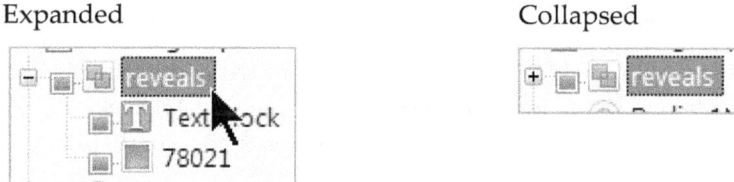

Tip 20: Two More Techniques to Make the Title Explorer More Readable

1. Arrange of objects in the Title Explorer in the order they appear from the top of the screen to the bottom because:

   - It speeds up development because it makes it easier to find things.

   - Screen readers read the text in that order.

   - When you export the course for translation, the text appears in this order.

   - When you export the course to MS Word®, the text appears in this order.

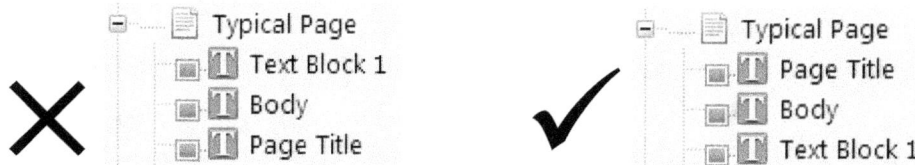

2. From time to time, right-click in the Title Explorer on the topmost line and select Collapse All. Then expand back to the area you were working on. This will keep you from getting lost.

Tip 21: Use the Lectora Placement Rules Effectively

When copying and pasting or inserting a Library object, Lectora inserts and places the object in most instances following these two rules:

Position on the Page (X,Y coordinates): Visible objects are positioned on the page in the **same location where** they were when they were saved. Be sure that your page is big enough to hold the objects. If you don't see them, select the object in the Title Explorer and check the X,Y coordinates at in the Status bar.

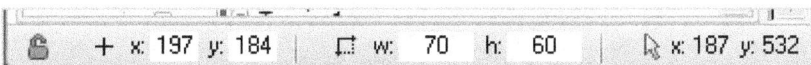

Location in the Title Explorer: The object is placed **immediately after** the object currently selected. So if you want a page to go *after* page 10, first click on page 10 in the left pane and then insert the Library object. If you want an object to be layered in front of square, select the square and insert the object. If you get it wrong, you can always drag and drop it to the right place.

Bottom line: Be sure you have the right object selected before inserting a new one.

Tip 22: Copy Objects Without Using the Clipboard

This does *not* use the clipboard so you can have one object copied to the clipboard while copying another.

- Click on the object in the Title Explorer.

- If you hold the Ctrl key down while dragging, a small + sign in a box will appear (Windows® standard) indicating you are making a copy, not moving the original.

Tip 23: How to Remember Pages You Need to Fix Later

Sometimes you may encounter a page and find you need more information or a graphic that is not currently available. One easy way to remember to come back here is to put a Note on the page.

Tools ribbon > Add Note.

This causes the page name in the Title Explorer to be in bold.

Later on, when you need to come back and fix these things, you can go to the Tools ribbon and print a Notes Report and see all the notes in the course.

D. Layout like a Pro

A big part of your work involves laying out each page. These tips help you do that quickly, effectively, and accurately. They cover things like a free screen ruler to use *between* applications, using guides, ideal page size, resizing and alignment techniques, and working with overlapping objects.

Tip 24: Use a Better Free Magnifier

Moving objects with precision can be a problem. While you can always use numeric calculations, the GUI age is here. When moving objects with precision on the screen, click on them and use the arrow keys.

One trick I learned when trying to line things up is that the Lectora magnification is not always precise down to the pixel level but the Windows® Magnifier is. Make a shortcut so you can get to it quickly. You can adjust the level of magnification (only zooms in, not out) and is extremely precise.

Tip 25: Working with Layers

How Lectora Decides Which Objects Are in Front

When a page is constructed by a browser (or rendering program) it puts items on the page *in the order that they appear in the* Title Explorer. As it starts to create the page from the information sent to it, it starts at the top of the Title Explorer and puts the objects on the page as it encounters them. This way the first items down end up behind the ones that come later.

Example: It's like cards off the top of a deck and dealing them out. The cards on the top of the deck go on the table first. They are covered up by the cards farther down the deck.

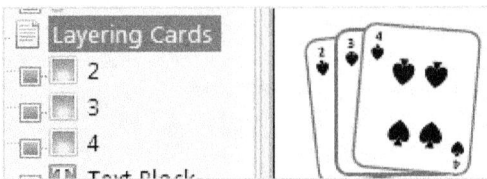

When a page is presented to the learner after publishing, two rendering passes over the Lectora content take place.

The **first** pass selects objects that do *not* have the Always on Top property checked.

Title level objects are placed on the screen beginning with the *top* in the Title Explorer.

- Assignable Unit objects go on top of them in the same sequence.
- Chapter level objects are next followed by Section and Page level objects.

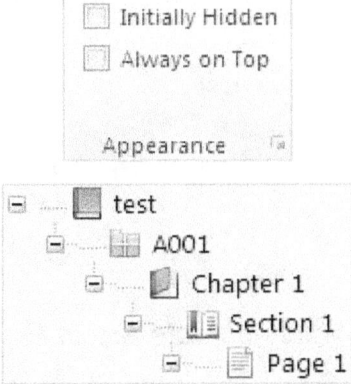

In the example shown here, the blue header appears behind both the Breadcrumb and the Course Title. If the Breadcrumb and the Course Title text blocks overlapped, the Course Title would be in front of the Breadcrumb. This way, if you have background objects for the Title or Chapter, any overlapping ones on the Page will appear in front of them.

Now, suppose you have some objects like navigation buttons at the Title level that you want to be sure are on top of things on the Page.

That is when you use the Always on Top property.

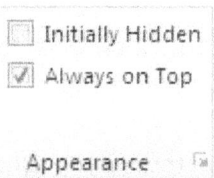

In the **second** pass, the rendering application selects objects that *do have* the Always On Top property checked. These objects are placed in front of any first pass objects in the same way as first pass objects were layered.

- Title level objects go on first from the top in the Title Explorer down to the first AU/Chapter/Section or Page.

- Assignable Unit objects go on top of them in the same sequence.

- Then Chapter level objects are next followed by Section level objects and then the objects on the page.

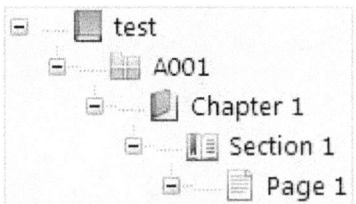

How You Can Control Which Objects Are in Front

To move object to the front or to the back within a given level (Title, AU, Chapter, Section, Page) you can do one of the following:

- Right click on the object and select the desired movement.

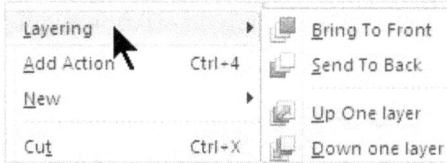

- In the Title Explorer, drag the object
  - up to move it *behind* other objects or
  - down to move it *in front of* other objects.

How to Work with Objects That Are Behind Other Objects

When you are working with the object on the front layer, it is easily visible. You can just click on it and do what needs to be done. But when you want to work with an object that is behind another one, you have to do something to bring it to the top to work on. This is when you use the Visibility Check Boxes.

The Visibility Check Box has three important uses:

- It allows you to hide objects on the page that might be getting in the way of what you are currently working on.

- If you are working on a page with objects that show or hide, then you can use this to kind of preview how things will appear.

- The hidden objects **don't print when you print the page from Lectora.**

1. To turn it on, select Preferences from the File ribbon.

2. Check the Show visibility check box.

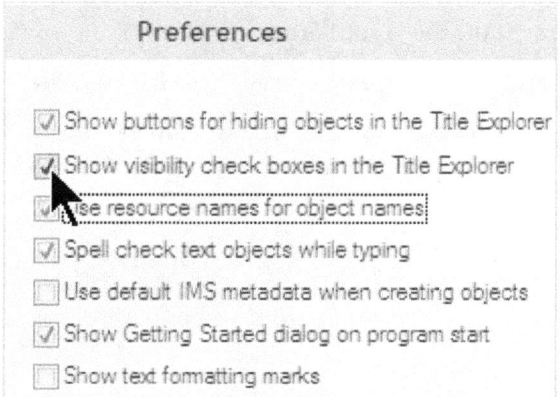

3. Clear the box to the left of the object in the Title Explorer. This will hide the object from view in the layout area so you can see the object behind it.

   This hides the object for editing purposes only. It will still appear on the screen when your course is run.

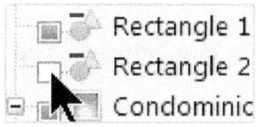

Tip 26: The Quickest Way to Lay Out a Page

New Lectora users sometimes forget this one. Use the guides under the View ribbon to easily create a consistent layout. Guides help you line objects up consistently and easily from page to page.

- To create a guide:

- Turn on Rulers using Ctrl+R or the View ribbon.

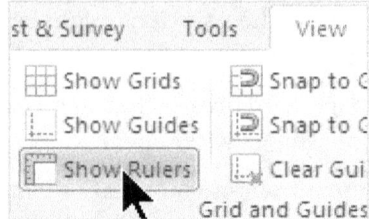

- Then click in the middle of ruler and drag it to where you want it.

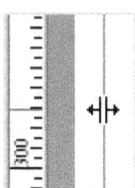

- To reposition a guide, hold the Ctrl key down, click on the guide, and drag.

- To delete one, drag it off the layout area.

- To quickly view and hide the guides, press Ctrl+E or use the View ribbon.

- They usually default to bright blue, but I like a silver color better. Change their color by clicking on the Options and then setting the Guides Color to some shade of gray.

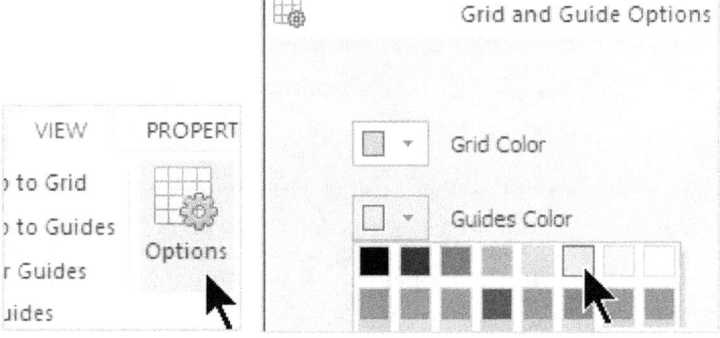

Warning 6: It is *not* enough just to have guides. You also need to have turned on Snap to Guides.

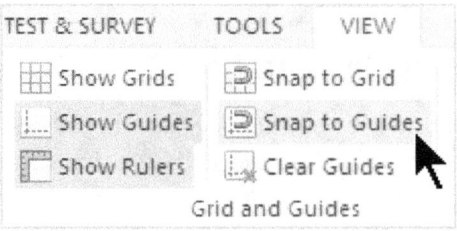

Tip 27: Tips for Using Snap-to Guides on All 4 Sides

There seems to be one gotcha here. If you have two parallel guides and drag an object that is just about the width between them to the top one, it is likely to stick to the *bottom* guide instead. This happened to me with one guide for the page title and another for the text blocks on the page. Sometimes when needing to move or resize the title block it kept aligning with the bottom guide instead of the top. Finally, I moved the bottom guide down a bit just to stop all the trouble.

Tip 28: How to Put the Page Back the Way It Will Be Viewed

After you have been working on a page for a while, the edit view in Lectora is not necessarily the way it will be seen. When you click on an object, it comes to the forefront so you can work on it. In the process, it covers the ones behind it. The Refresh tool puts all the objects back to their respective layers. You can activate Refresh from the View menu or by pressing the F5 key.

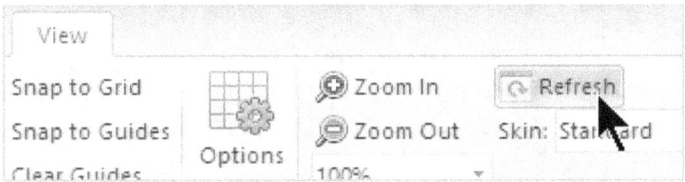

Tip 29: How to Keep the Background Image from Repeating

It appears that the easiest way to keep it from repeating is to make it the same size as the page specified in the title. If it is different, frequently it will repeat. If you are unwilling to resize the image then, create an HTML object at the title level so it will be on all pages. You can shrink it down so it does not get in the way of your design. It is only a placeholder.

Insert an HTML Extension from the Insert ribbon.

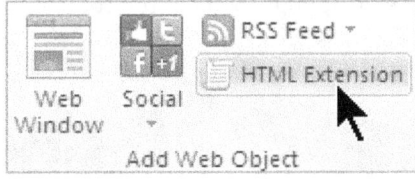

On its Properties ribbon, click Edit.

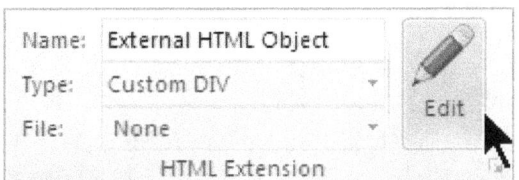

Enter this:

```
<style text="text/css">
body { background-repeat:no-repeat; } </style>
```

Tip 30: Select a Visually Appealing Page Alignment

Make your page alignment centered, as it will look a bit better if the user changes the size of the browser window. This usually is not a factor when courses are running from an LMS, but when they are published to Web (HTML), it can matter.

On the Design ribbon, select Centered from the HTMP Page Alignment.

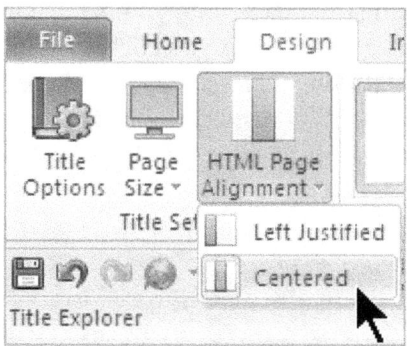

Tip 31: Optimal Maximum Page Size

A 1024 x 768 screen has about 995 x 595 maximum in a browser with three toolbars showing at the top and a status bar at the bottom.

Remember that while you can make the screen 995 wide, you will be able to print much less than that. With the default settings of .75 in on each margin, you can only print about 670 in portrait mode and 910 in landscape mode. So if you plan to print your screens, then keep this in mind.

Given all this, set the page size at 900 x 600 so that it all shows on the screen and can be printed.

Tip 32: Page Flashing Bothering You in HTML?

If it is, then turn on some kind of transition on the Design ribbon.

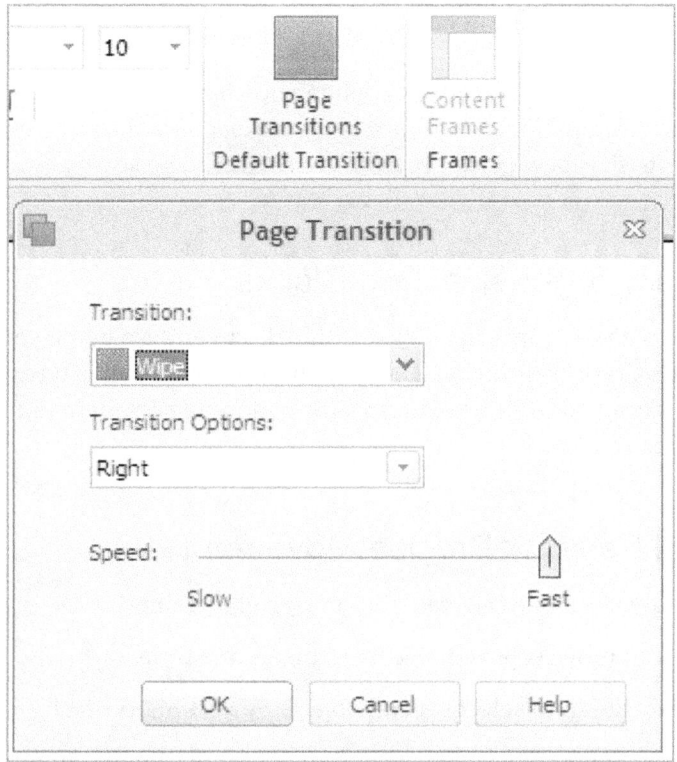

Tip 33: How to Work on a Page While Viewing the Original Version

Sometimes you want to work on one page while looking at another one or even the original version of this page. You can open a second copy of the title but you may be bitten by this approach. The best way is to navigate to the page you want to view and click the **Preview in Browser** button. Now you have that page in a separate window. Adjust your screen so you can see both this page and Lectora.

Tip 34: Tips for Using Make Objects the Same Width and/or Height

While this is a powerful tool all by itself, you can achieve some easy layout symmetry if you combine it with the Space Horizontal and Space Vertical. These Spacing commands frequently do a better job if all the objects are the same height if you are spacing vertically or same width if you are spacing horizontally. So, get them the right height or width first and then space.

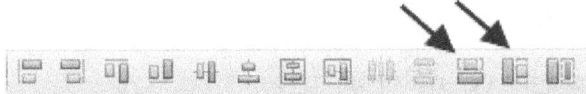

Note: it seems the rule here is the first object selected rules in terms of the size.

 **Warning 7:** Sometimes but not always, when you change the size of an image, it may look fine in Lectora but *distort when published and viewed using a browser.* So, if you do change its size, be sure to Preview in Browser to be sure.

Tip 35: Easily Right-size Text Blocks

For a variety of reasons, sometimes the text block can end up being smaller than the text requires. This results in missing text when published. You can resize the text block using its sizing handles or you can simply double click in it and it will expand downward to the right size.

Tip 36: Use Keys for Precise Movement

Use the arrow keys to move selected objects 1 pixel at a time.

Use Shift+arrow to move selected objects 10 pixels at a time.

Hold the Ctrl key down to select several objects by clicking on each.

Hold the Shift key down when dragging to restrict dragging to either horizontal or vertical movement.

Tip 37: How to Precisely Change an Object's Location or Size without the Position & Size Ribbon

Use the Status Bar at the bottom or your Lectora window. It is very handy for customizing the games that have moving objects. You can read precisely and set coordinates right in the Status Bar.

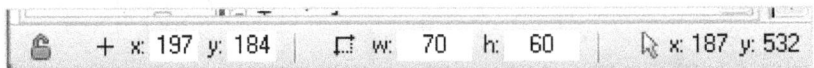

Tip 38: How to Design and Use a Color Scheme

Using a well-crafted color scheme in your course makes it more pleasing to the eye and more professional looking. (From chapter 2 of Designing Effective eLearning: A Step-by-Step Guide.)

If you have a logo or existing website, start with that. Keep the number of different colors to three or four.

Select a combination of colors that work well together. Some websites provide color scheme generators. The one I like best is www.colorschemedesigner.com. Just click on the RGB, enter your primary color, and then click in the schemes at the top left to see different combinations. You can search the internet for other color scheme generators if you don't like this one.

Lectora used to show the colors at the cursor position, but no more! Sigh! Using just Lectora, the only way I know of now to get the color codes is to use the eyedropper.

1. First, paste some graphic that has the desired colors in it. If it is too big or not usable, then do the following.

2. Create two or three text blocks at the Title level. Make them somewhat small and position them at the top of the screen. Group them and make the group Always on Top and Initially Hidden.

3. Now set the background color of each to the colors you want using the color selector.

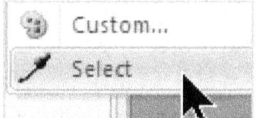

Tip 39: How to Use Change Contents to Simplify Page Layout

Many of you are aware that you can change the contents of a text box with an action. You see it done in the actions created by the Page Numbering tool.

In these examples, the New Contents can be

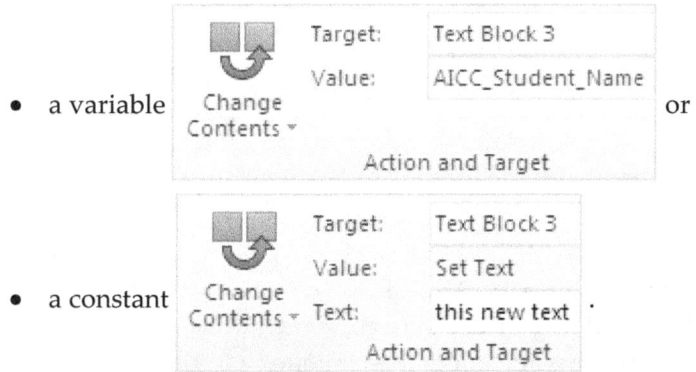

- a variable   or

- a constant

What many are not aware of is that you can also change the contents for *images and audio*. This is particularly useful when using graphics for something like status – not started, started, complete. Instead of having three images that you have to keep aligned, you only have **one**. It makes page layout much easier. Notice in the example here the New Contents is another graphic.

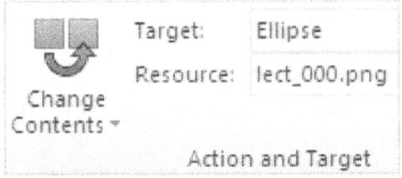

 **Warning 8:** When replacing graphics, all the graphics should be the *same size* or you will get some distortion. If your graphics are different sizes and you want to use this technique, then put the smaller ones on a white background the same size as the largest one and create a new graphic.

Warning 9: If you do text, know that the spell checker does not check the text as of Lectora 11.

Tip 40: How to Solve Problems with Overlapping Objects

Sometimes you have one object that covers another completely and when the learner does something, the covered/hidden one appears. *During testing,* it is good practice to offset them a little. You may have difficulty figuring out if it is showing at the right time or if it is just covered up or some other cause. Offset the top item a bit so you can see a portion of the bottom when you are testing the page. When it works, then line them up properly.

In this example, the grayed-out Next button is to cover the active Next button. During testing, they are offset as shown. In production, the gray one covers the black one.

E. Making Your Own Reusable Learning Objects

The most obvious way to create a reusable learning object (RLO) is to take an existing object and save it to your Lectora Library. This section covers how to do that effectively and avoid its pitfalls. Unfortunately, there are some limitations with Library objects that can be overcome by using another technique.

Let's begin with things you need to do *before* you save a Library object.

Tip 41: Prepare RLOs to Be Easier to Change

One of the most common RLOs I create is click to reveal. The learner is instructed to click on buttons to reveal more information. Instead of simply having the Show action show the desired text object, when I build an RLO, I put the text to be revealed in a group even if there is only one text block.

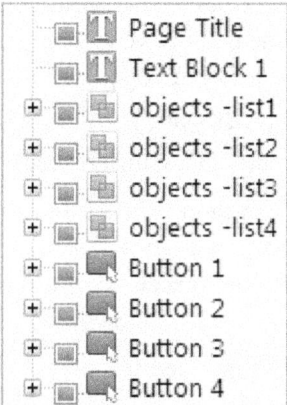

Why? Because when I go to reuse this, it may turn out that I want to show more than just one text block. Maybe this time it is a text block and a graphic. Maybe next time it is three pictures. I create a group for each button. If I show and hide groups instead of individual objects, then when I reuse it, all I have to do is replace the objects in the group. I do *not* have to change any actions or remember to set the Initially Hidden property. The work goes a lot faster and is much less prone to errors.

Tip 42: Prepare Text Block RLOs with Paragraph and Line Spacing

Lectora has styles but unfortunately, line spacing and paragraph spacing are not yet part of a Style. Here is a way around that.

1. Create a text block or page with several text blocks.

2. Enter some text in each and set the desired font, line spacing, and paragraph spacing.

3. Add a couple of blank spaces and then delete all the visible text.

4. Now save this as a Library object or put it in your Development chapter (covered soon).

Tip 43: Prepare RLOs with Meaningful Names

While this is not absolutely necessary, these tips will make your RLOs more usable because you may well forget what they are for or how it all works.

- Clearly label each image, text box, action, etc.

- For those objects where Lectora creates the variable name (questions and form objects), change them to be unique and easy to find. Lectora will **not** rename a variable if it is **not** already in use. i.e. it will use your variable name the first time. Then what you do is open the question or form object properties and change it to something unique in that title. Lectora will change all references to your variable name. Then you can bring in another copy of that Library object.

  - I recommend variable names like _Qx or _LibQx, which you will change when you use the object later. The underscore makes it easy to find later.

- Flag objects that need to be changed (like the ones that have special variable names or maybe need a condition changed) with special names. Making an arrow is one good way to make the object stand out and remind you that it needs to be changed Examples:

Question <-----------------------chg var

Check Answer Button < ================= chg condition

- Of course, you can also add Notes if the RLO is a Lectora page or higher.

Tip 44: Create Your Own Tools in a Development Chapter

This method has advantages over the Lectora library as well as disadvantages.

Add a chapter at the end of the course to hold all your standard pages like a typical content page (maybe several layouts), an exercise page, a video page, an audio page, etc. Create the standard text blocks and enter a couple of blank spaces and apply the desired style. Then you can copy and paste these pages or objects on them as needed.

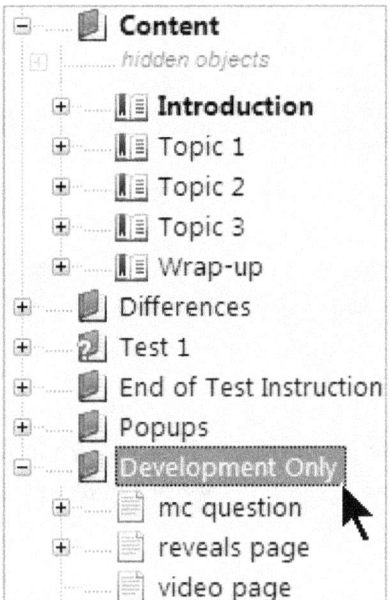

One advantage over a library is that the actions can reference title level objects and will still be valid when copied. The disadvantage is that to use something in this chapter, you first have to move over to it and copy it, then move back to where you were and paste. I little bit more work but may be worth it for objects that reference global items.

Tip 45: Put Your RLO in the Lectora Library and Access It from There

Most any object or set of objects you use in Lectora can be saved as a Library object and then reused in future courses.

- A graphic image

- A single text block

- Several text blocks and images selected together

- A group of objects

- An action or several actions

- A page or several pages

- A section, chapter, title

- Lots more

You can*not* create a library object from a *part* of a question.

To create Lectora Library object, all you have to do is right click on the object or one of the objects selected and select Save as Library Object.

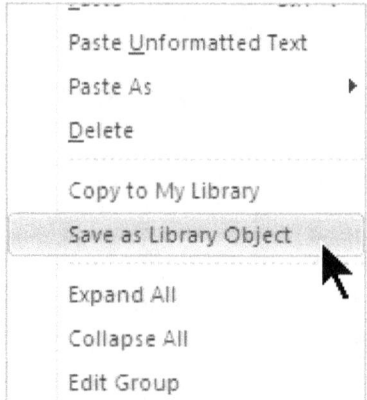

Then when you want to use it again, just click on My Library on the right side of the Lectora window and double click on the library object you want to add to your course.

Now that is the good news. There are a number of cautions you need to know about.

Tip 46: Lectora Library Cautions and Limitations

The following is not to be considered a complete list of considerations but should keep you from making some of the more common mistakes.

Warning 10: Do not use any of the prohibited characters for a Windows® file name (/*?:<>|.) used in the name of the first object.

 **Warning 11:** The worst one and most common is using a colon (:). You get NO WARNING that it could not save it. It acts like it saved it. Therefore, best practice here is to check right after you save one and be sure it is there. If not, check the name.

 **Warning 12: Variable Names:** While you can save questions and form objects, know that when they are reused later they will create a *new variable name if the one in the library object is already in use.* There is a workaround for this discussed later. Examples:

– You save a drop-down list box and the variable name is DropList_0001. Later you use it again in the same title. Lectora will assign it a new variable name, DropList_0002 if you have no other drop-down list boxes.

– You save a multiple-choice question with the variable name of QA. Later you use that same question twice in a new title. The first time it will use the variable name of QA. The second time you use it, Lectora will change the variable name to Question_0xxx, where xxx is the next available question number.

 **Warning 13: Lectora keeps its library objects where they may not be backed up.**

You can determine where Lectora is saving the library objects by going to File ribbon > Preferences.

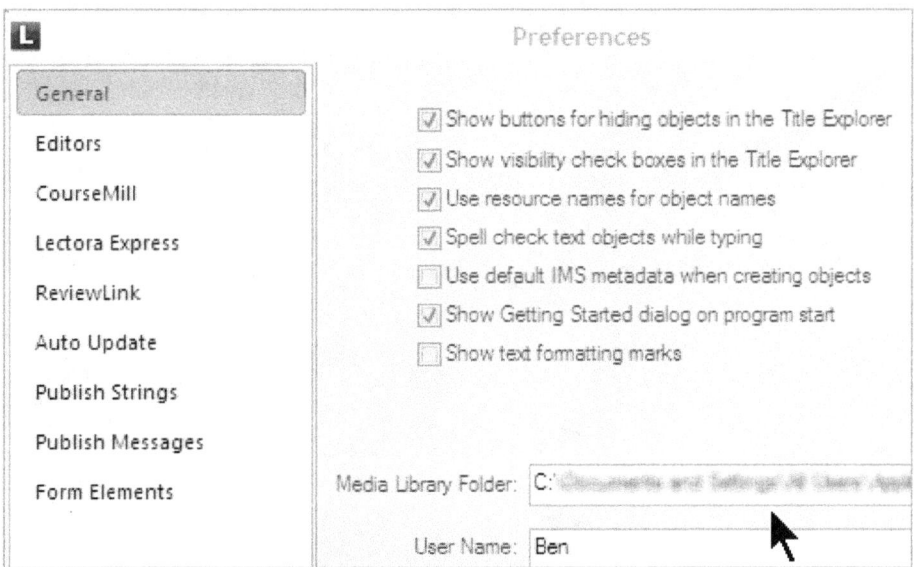

This may be not one of the folders you normally back up so be sure to have your backup software find this folder if you use it.

Warning 14: Actions Referencing Objects: You may have actions in your Library object that reference objects not in the object like popup pages, hiding the Next button, or running an action group at the title level. When you insert the Library object the next time, all these references are broken. Your best alternative here is to put your RLO in the course itself in the Development chapter (discussed later).

Tip 47: How to Access Your Library Faster

While you can access the Lectora Library by clicking on it on the left side of the window, I have found that with two screens, there is a faster way.

1. First, navigate to the Library folder using the information in Preferences.

2. Then create a shortcut to your Library folder and put it on the desktop or somewhere you can get to it quickly.

3. When you need to use a Library Objects, just open the folder and drag and drop the object onto your layout area.

F. Your Notes

When you find things that will speed up your development, make a note of them here.

2. Power Tips for Specific Objects

This chapter covers tips associated with specific kinds of objects (text blocks, buttons, tables, graphics, menus, etc.). Don't try to read them all. Instead, when you start to use one of the objects mentioned, read that section.

A. Text Tips

This section focuses on text with tips on how to set and retain formatting. Following sections deal with special topics like Tables and Bullets.

Controlling Text Formatting

Tip 48: Automating the Text Formatting

Well, most of you probably know this, but just in case, use the Lectora Text Styles to set your text formats. If you need to change it, say from Arial to Verdana, then all you need do is change the style and reply Yes to the question it will ask and all instances of that text will change.

You create styles with these steps.

1. Click on or in a text block and then click the down arrow on Text Style on the Home ribbon.

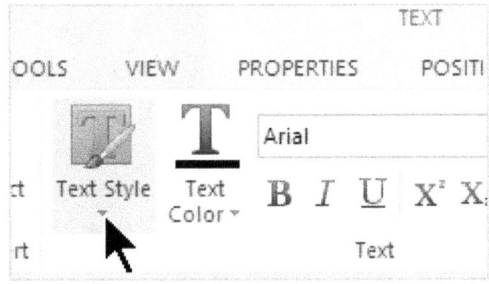

2. Select Manage Styles from the dropdown list.

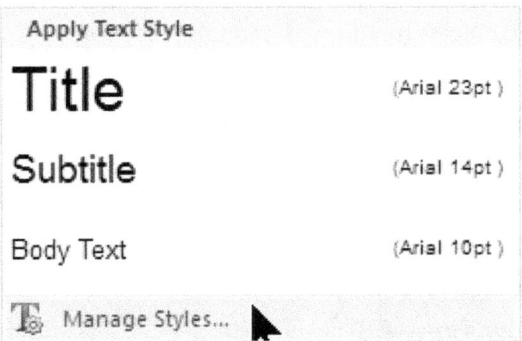

3. Then just click New and create your desired style. You can come back any time and change it by clicking on the style and then the Edit button.

 **Warning 15:** However, unlike MS Word, the styles are *not* coded below the surface with hidden codes. What that means is that if you have two styles that are the same but different names and you change one, it will change all the text using either text style.

 **Warning 16:** Further, unlike MS Word, it will not change text with any formatting modification like bold, italics, or a different color.

Maybe we need an example here. Say you had a MS Word document that used these two styles. You have used the first for the labels on all your pictures and the second on all your tables.

Style   **Example**

- Picture Label: 10 pt Arial   "Picture of *inside* gear"

- Table Label: 10 pt Arial   "**Inside** Gear Table"

Now you decide that you want your Table Labels to be 12 pt Arial bold. So, you go into MS Word and change the style and it changes all the Table labels without asking. You do the same thing in Lectora and click Yes when it asks you if you want to change all of them. Here is what it looks like now.

MS Word	Lectora
Picture of *inside* gear	Picture of *inside* gear
Inside Gear Table	Inside Gear Table
MS Word *did not change* any text using the same specifications like the Picture Label style. It was able to do this because behind the scenes, it uses hidden codes to remember which style is in use.	Lectora changed *all* the text that was 10 pt Arial *regardless* of style used. So you can see it changed the Picture Labels too!
MS Word did change *all* the text using the Table Label style *including text with any additional text formatting you had added to it like italic or bold.*	Lectora did *not* change any text that had any additional formatting applied like italic or bold.

As long as we are on the subject of differences, as of today Lectora 11, Lectora styles do *not* incorporate paragraph spacing, line spacing, or any kind of indentation, borders, highlighting, or background color whereas you can do all that and more in MS Word.

Tip 49: How to Globally Change Text That Has Additional Formatting Applied

When you change a style in Lectora, you will get a question asking you if you want to change all occurrences of that style. If you say Yes, it will replace everything that is *exactly* that style. So, as we said above, it will not change the bold and italicized text. Here are two options beyond simply manually looking for the places that need change.

Option 1: Use This If You Have a Lot to Change

1. Create a style matching the text that was not changed. In the previous example, you would create one for 10 pt Arial Bold and one for 10 pt Arial Italics.

2. Then change the style to 12 pt. and reply Yes to the question. Now it will change all the 10 pt bold text to 12 pt bold.

Option 2: Use This If You Have Some But They Are Hard to Find

Export the course to MS Word (File > Export > Word). Then open that and use Advanced Find on the Home ribbon in MS Word to search for the font size that may not have been changed.

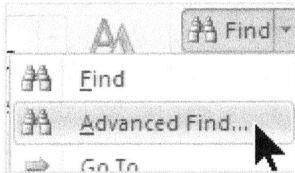

You still have to change them manually in Lectora.

Tip 50: Getting Your Styles to Another Lectora User

Another bummer around styles is that if you send your title to someone else who does not have your styles, *they* will not have them. MS Word embeds the styles in the document. Not so with Lectora. The text will retain its formatting but the person you sent it to will not have the styles to apply or change. So, for example, say you took over the maintenance of some Lectora courses after someone else left your company. Since the styles are *not* part of the title, you will not have them to apply or change. Here is what you need to do *before* that person leaves.

1. Open Lectora and find a text block.

2. Click on it and select Manage Styles from the dropdown Text Styles button.

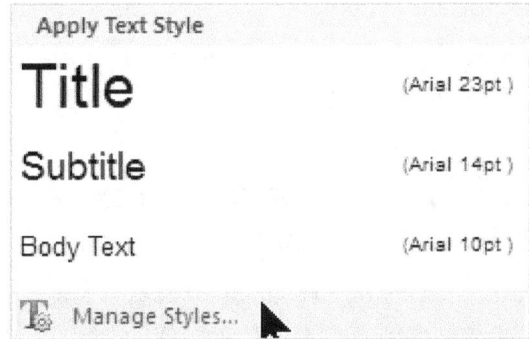

3. Hold the Ctrl key down and click on the styles you want to export.

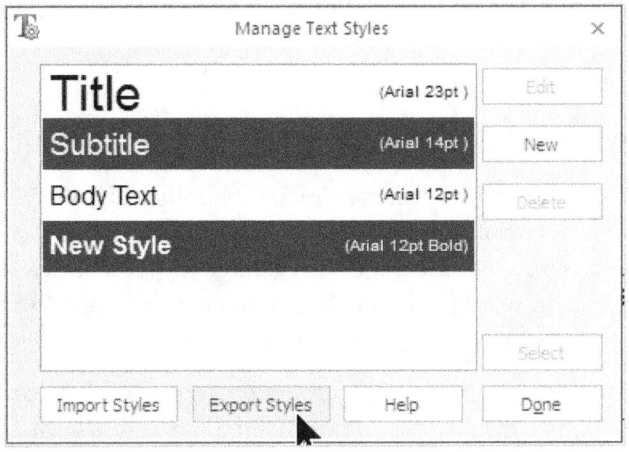

4. Then click the Export Styles button.

5. Put that file on your computer, go to this same window, and click Import Styles. It will add those you do not have and replace the ones you do.

Tip 51: How to Retain Text Format of the Target Text Block when Pasting

If you paste unformatted, you frequently lose the formatting of the text block (font size, color, bold, italic, justification, paragraph and line spacing) if *all* the text is replaced. To avoid this, put one blank space in the text block, and format it as desired (color, size, bold …) Then when you paste, don't replace all, just click in front of the space and paste unformatted.

Tip 52: Tips on Using the Text Highlighter

This is a nice alternative to bold or italic. Like all fancy features, this is a nice new addition **but don't over use it**. You will get the best results if you come up with a standard for your courses and use it in the same way throughout. This will alert the learner to the really important material.

Also, keep in mind that red/green color blindness is the most frequently occurring when selecting colors for highlighting.

Tip 53: How to Control the Format of Text Where a Change Contents Action Is Used

If you use a Change Contents action to change what appears in a text box, you have limited control over the font size, face, color, and style (bold, italic). It takes on the format of the first character. You only get one choice. Use the previous technique of formatting a blank space to set the formatting to something other than the page default.

Tip 54: How to Control the Format of Text in an Entry Field

Is there anyway (within Lectora) to manipulate the following attributes of an entry field such as font type (Arial, Verdana, etc.), font size, and font color? Yes. The entry field picks up the attributes of the page so you have to work backwards. Set the font face, size, and color you want the entry field to have in the Page Properties. Then reformat the text blocks on the page the way you want them.

If you want to suppress the entry field borders or right justify the text, see *Lectora 301: Techniques for Professionals* available from Amazon in late 2014.

Tip 55: Best Practice for Importing Text from Other Sources

Warning 17: If you don't know already, it is generally a **very bad idea** to copy and simply paste text from another application directly into Lectora. When you use a simple copy and paste of text from another application, you run the risk of copying in all kinds of hidden formatting. This hidden formatting does not always work well in Lectora. Or, even worse, when you viewed from a browser lots of things look different – you have new bullets where there are none in Lectora, spacing is all off, etc.

Here is the text as it looked in MS Word captured with SnagIt.

> • Lowes/Home Depot/ Dollar Tree
>   – Oak blinds 31 x 53; door 21.5 x 35.5 with 1.25 frame
>   – Basement lights
>   – Light switches

Now, here it is when I pasted it in as a text block in Lectora. I turned on the Show Text Formatting Marks and put an Outline around the Text Block so you could see more clearly. The bullets have all changed but still there is no indication of any hidden characters.

> _ Lowes/Home·Depot/·
>   Dollar·Tree¶
>   . Oak·blinds·31·x·53;·
>   door·21.5·x·35.5·with·
>   1.25·frame¶
>   . Basement·lights¶
>   . Light·switches¶

Now, here it is when viewed in IE 8. Notice that some hidden characters now appear, the text runs all the way to the right, and the text is cut off at the bottom.

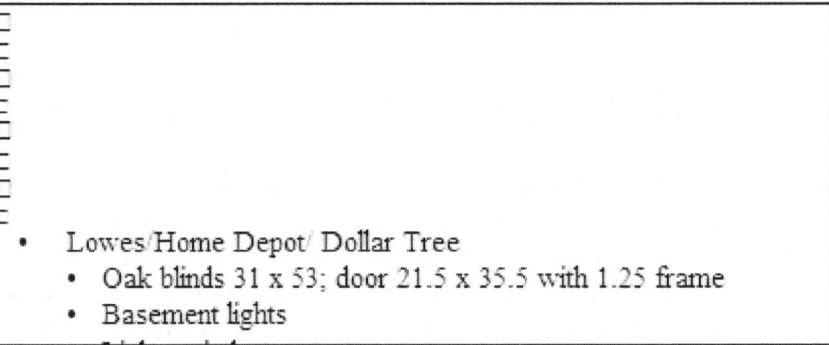

Instead of just pasting, either:

- Paste Unformatted or

- Paste into Notepad first and then copy and paste into Lectora.

If you have a lot of text going into different text boxes, you may find it easier to use the second option as you do not have to manually select Paste Unformatted or use Ctrl+Shift+V to paste.

Tip 56: Best Practice Using Special Fonts

Warning 18: If you use special fonts that are not generally available, when your course is viewed by someone who does not have those fonts, the browser will substitute another similar font. The spacing may not be what you expect.

If you are not sure all users of your course will have all the fonts you used, make the text blocks where the special fonts appear "Convert To Image." Lectora will generate images and the user will not have to have the font on their machine.

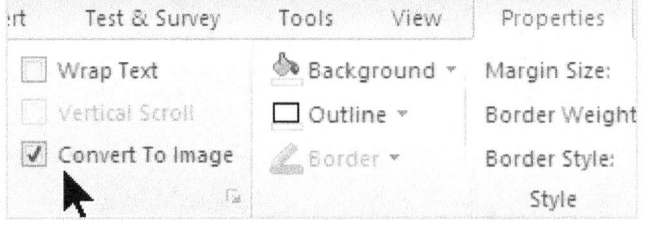

Tip 57: Pros and Cons of Convert To Image

There are several downsides to Convert To Image. Before you go jumping in and using this option on all text blocks, consider these points:

Advantages

- The primary advantage is that the text blocks don't resize when published.

- Non-standard fonts are readable on all machines and look pretty close to the original except for being a graphic instead of text.

- Bullets are bigger.

Disadvantages

- One is that it creates GIFs and they take a bit longer to load than plain text. If you have a lot of them, possibly could affect performance.

- It is not 508 Compliant – i.e. text readers cannot read them.

- It makes the HTML files *not* searchable. If you leave them as text, you can use a search engine to search your text files. Sometimes when I know I have a page that contains some text but cannot remember which page in some 50 lessons it is in, I just run a Windows® search on the HTML folder and look for the word in the pages.

- The learner cannot copy the text from the browser window. I had one client who had lost the original source and all the text boxes were rendered as an image. He had to retype them all instead of copying and pasting.

Controlling Text Block Layout

Tip 58: Copying Paragraph and Line Spacing from One Paragraph to Another

Lectora as yet has no Format Painter as you find in MS Word or PowerPoint®. If you want to copy paragraph and line spacing from one paragraph to another, just copy and paste the hidden paragraph spacing.

1. First, click after the last punctuation in a properly formatted paragraph.

2. Drag right and you will get what looks like a blank space. It should turn black.

> ## Test changing style█
>
> this line **bold** *italic*

3. Copy.

4. Select the same area on a paragraph where you want the same spacing.

5. Paste.

The target paragraph will now have the same spacing as the copy-from one.

Tip 59: How to Get *Smooth* Text Block Transitions

When you use transitions with text blocks, frequently they will transition in and look grainy. Here are three things you can try to make them look better.

- Option 1: Give the text box a background, white or the color of the page background, then the fuzziness disappears. Looks great!

- Option 2: If that does not work with your desired browser, then check the property on the text block to Convert To Image. Note that this may make bullets a little bigger than otherwise.

- Option 3: Cover the text block with a graphic that matches the background (usually a small white GIF stretched to cover the text block. Use a transition *out* instead of *in*.

Tip 60: How to *Vertically* Center Text

Use a table with one cell. Set the Cell Alignment to center. See also the following section on Tables.

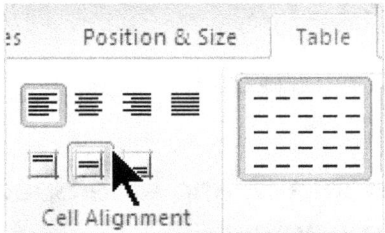

Tip 61: Managing Wrap-Around for Text Blocks

Be sure to put your objects **in front of** the wrapping text box. Don't just check the Always on Top property as you may need it later for other objects. Instead, right click on the object and select Layering > Bring to Front.

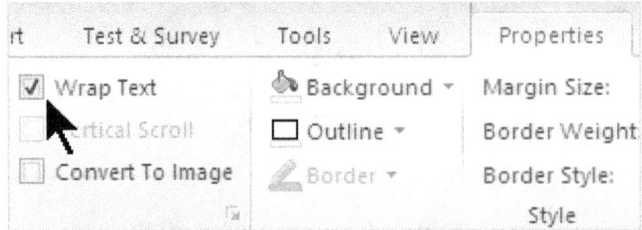

Other Text Block Tricks

Tip 62: How to Have Common Text

If you want the *same* text to appear in multiple places in a title, a popup page does not do the job. If you want a single source for the text, like maybe a case study description, so can make changes in one place and have them reflected everywhere here are some choices:

- Place the text box at a title, chapter, or section level and inherit (this may require disinheriting and you can only have the text in one position on the page)

- Insert a document (.txt or .RTF) that contains the desired text. Unfortunately, this means you will have a border around it.

- Create it externally and save as a graphic. Then insert the graphic into Lectora. As long as the graphic remains the same size, you can replace it with a new one and all instances of the graphic will be changed.

- Create a Flash object with a scrolling text box using FlyPaper. Or you can do something rough using Snap!

Tip 63: How to Standardize Text Imported from PowerPoint®

Have you ever seen a PowerPoint® presentation where the font sizes and styles were all over the globe? The Translation Tool can save hours of time and wear and tear on your mouse to bring the text into some kind of uniformity.

After importing the PowerPoint® file into Lectora, click on the Tools ribbon and then Translation Tool and create an RTF file of all the text.

Open the .RTF file in WordPad (do **not** use MS Word), select the desired text and change the font style to whatever style you want to use, save the file and import it back into your title. All the font characteristics you changed are now shown in the Lectora title.

Thanks to Ghughes on the Lectora forum.

Warning 19: The Translation Tool is a powerful and potentially dangerous tool. Be sure to read the chapter on Tips for Using the Translations Tool later in this book.

Tip 64: Positioning to a Spot in Scrolling Text Blocks

When you need this trick, you really need it – **the ability to scroll to a particular place in a scrolling text box.** Insert an object (white, transparent, or maybe even a picture/graphic) where you want to be able to scroll. Then on the Go To actions you just specify the desired object in the text box and it jumps right there.

One word of caution - when you leave and then return to this text box, it may look distorted – as if maybe the graphics are out of place. Preview it in *Browser* before making any changes.

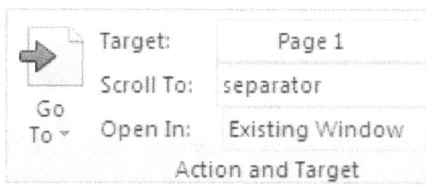

But, see the next tip.

Tip 65: Heads up When Using Graphics in Text Blocks

A while back Lectora introduced the capability to put graphics in text blocks. Generally, it works fine although when used in long scrolling text blocks it sometimes looks a little squirrely.

Warning 20: Sometimes those graphics inside text blocks suddenly all end up at the beginning of the block. This seems to happen only on rare occasions and I think if you import from a translation file.

The workaround is to group text and graphics together and use that approach instead of embedding the graphics inside the text blocks.

Tip 66: Real-time Spell Checking

Warning 21: Lectora does *not* flag misspelled words *unless* your cursor is actually inside the text block.

Warning 22: Lectora does *not* flag misspelled words when the text is changed using a Change Contents action.

If it is not, then there is no indication of a spelling error so a word to the wise. Spell check your entire document when you are through. Spell Check is found on the Tools ribbon.

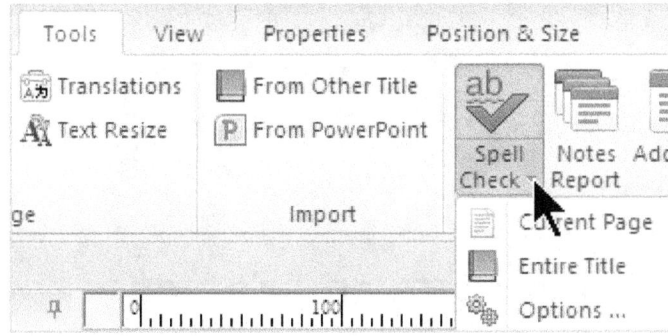

Tip 67: High-speed Find

When using Find in long titles, it can take a long time for the Lectora to find what you are looking for. If you need to do several searches, either

- export your course to MS Word using File ribbon > Export > Word

or

- the Translation tool under the Tools ribbon.

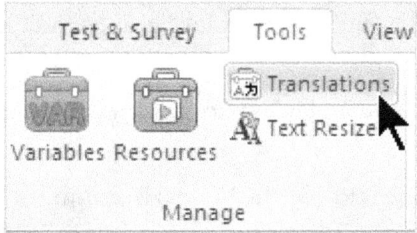

Then you can open the exported file with MS Word and find what you need.

Tip 68: Finding Text Changes in Different Versions of a Course

Either export both the old and new versions of your course to MS Word using File ribbon > Export > Word or the Translation tool under the Tools ribbon. Then open MS Word and, on the Review ribbon, select Compare to compare the two documents. This will flag all the text changes in the two versions.

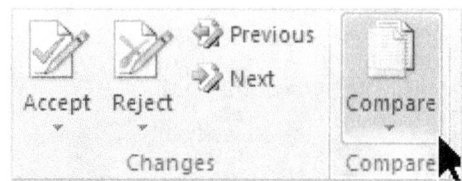

B. Working with Bullets and Tables

Bullets and tables are really part of the text topic but they have such special needs, I thought I would put them together so you could find them quicker. There are tips here on how to do things a little quicker, how to do things that you can't do the normal way like special bullets, and how to fix problems.

Tip 69: How to Insert Blank Lines after Bulleted or Numbered Lines

Position the cursor at the end of the last line. Then simply hold the shift key down and press enter to get a blank line. It is a lot faster than turning bullets on and off and another nice thing is that it keeps the numbering going.

Tip 70: How to Fix Unwanted Different Color Bullets

Sometimes the bullet will be a different color because the first or last character on the line is that color.

- One workaround is to add a blank space and make it the color you want the bullet to be.

- Another is to use a table and put the bullets in column 1 and the text in column 2.

Tip 71: How to Fix Unwanted Different Size Bullets

Occasionally you will have the last bullet in a text block be larger or smaller than the rest. The safe way to correct this is to click in the text block, select all, and then change the font size. Then re-apply any other formatting needed.

Tip 72: How to Easily Insert Rows or Columns in Tables

Fast way to insert a row in the middle of a table is to copy one and then click at the beginning of a row and paste. It is faster than navigating your way through the Insert Row maze.

Columns work the same way.

Tip 73: How to Get Top and Bottom Cell Margins

I am not sure why, but the cell margins in Lectora are only on the left and the right, not the top and bottom of the cell.

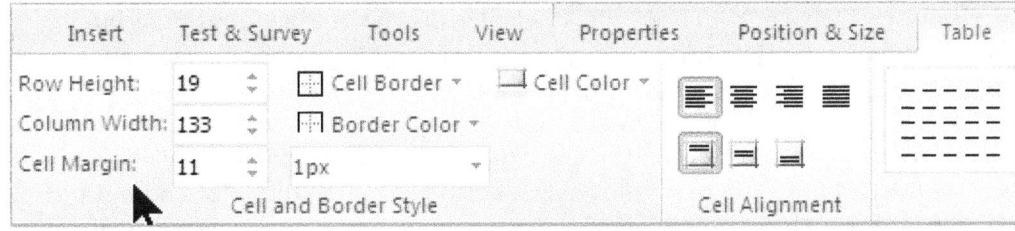

If you want the effect of margins at the top and bottom of a cell, you have to use Paragraph Spacing available from Right click > Paragraph > Paragraph Spacing or on the Home ribbon.

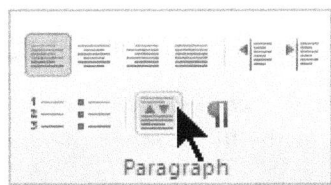

The good news that this looks fine when published to HTML or SCORM. The bad news is that it does not when viewed in Lectora or published to an executable. Here I added 5 points before and after the paragraph in the first cell. You will notice a white band at the top of the first cell. Compare it to the second cell as well as to how it looks in HTML.

Lectora: IE8:

	second cell
First cell	

	second cell
First cell	

C. Working with Graphics

Graphics have their own set of issues. If you are not careful, you can create much larger than necessary image folders, the wrong kind of graphics that work in Lectora but don't in HTML, or you can end up with many copies of the same image. There are also tips on how to get your work done faster.

Tip 74: Use the Right Color Code

Warning 23: Sometimes graphics that use the CMYK (Cyan, Magenta, Yellow, blacK) color scheme instead of RBG (Red, Blue, Green) will not display correctly in a browser. I have not yet been able to narrow down the exact conditions but it seems to happen rarely with courses viewed from an LMS rather than simply viewed from the desktop.

The fix seems to be fairly easy if you have the right tool. My graphic artist just opened the JPG in PhotoShop, clicked on a button changing the color-coding, and saved it. You may be able to do that with PowerPoint® too. Just paste into Power-Point® and then right click and Save As a different file format (if it was a JPG, then save as PNG). I have not tried this, just a guess.

Tip 75: How to Speed Up Inserting Graphics

Open your image folder (or any other one where you keep graphics) and make it one column wide so you can see the full name of the graphics. Place it on one side of your screen.

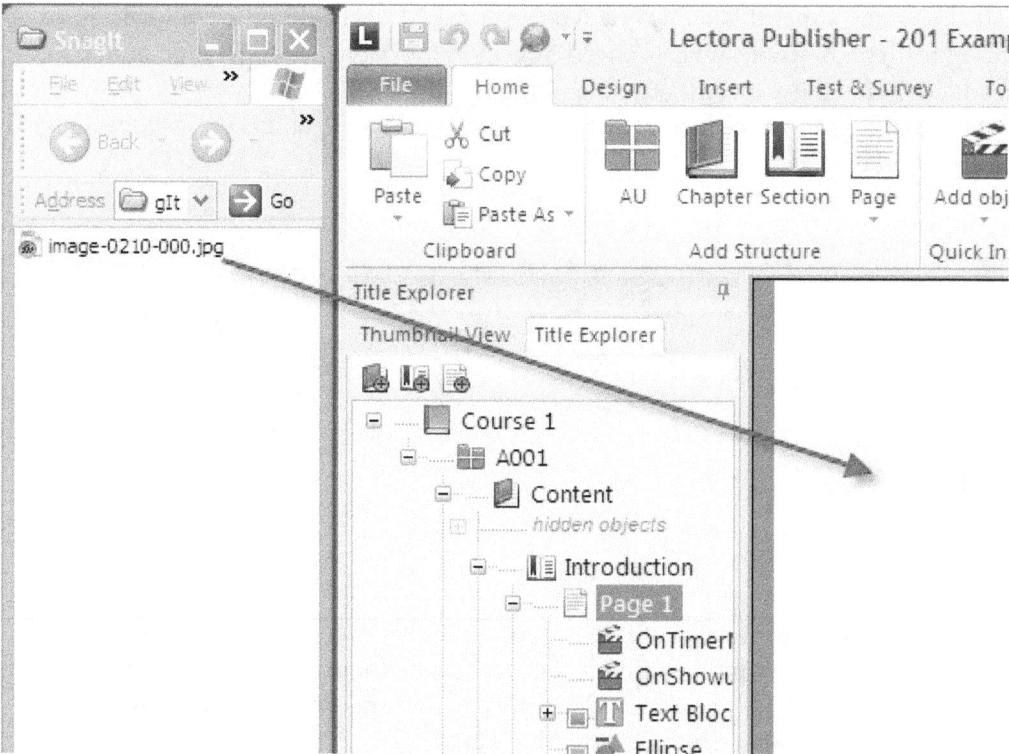

Anytime you create a new graphic with an outside tool (Photoshop, Flash, Fireworks, SnagIt) put the image directly in the images folder. New images always appear at the end of the folder when it is open. Then you can just drag and drop it on to your Lectora page instead of going through the many-click process of using a ribbon.

Note: This does *not* work for Lectora Online last time I checked.

Tip 76: Getting at the Source Images in PowerPoint®

Sometimes you need to get at the source pictures used in a PowerPoint® storyboard sent to you by a client. Here is what you do.

1. Copy the PowerPoint® file.

2. Change the file type of the *copy* to **.zip**.

3. Open and look around. Somewhere you will find all the original source images for the pictures and background images. Try the Media folder first.

Tip 77: Best Practice for Different Graphic File Types

The Lectora User Guide has more information but here is a quick summary for people new to web development. NOTE: Lectora does some sort of compression on most all images going to HTML. Not sure about single file executable. These are generalizations and as with anything, there are exceptions. Different formats take up different amounts of space. Bit map formatted objects (BMP) can take as much as 50 times the space as a JPG, PNG, or a GIF – 500KB vs 10KB. This can have a significant impact on how quickly your pages display. Whenever possible use one of these three rather than a bitmap.

GIF   Usually takes less space on the disk, can have transparent areas, but is **not** as good for pictures. Use GIFs whenever you can if they display well on the target monitor.

JPG   This format is great for pictures. Be careful when resizing. They cannot have transparent areas; sometimes end up with 1 px black line on one or more sides in Lectora for some reason.

PNG   A newer format than JPG, PNGs are great for pictures. Use PNG 32 format when creating if you want transparent areas. They frequently can cause a big problem in IE 6 – if the image itself is not rectangular there may be pale blue where there is no picture.

Tip 78: What to Do About Big Graphics

Lectora gives you warnings if your graphics are large implying that they might take a long time to download. However, when it publishes them to some form of HTML, it frequently, but not always, shrinks them. If you have some large graphics and are concerned, publish your title and then look in the html>images folder for your graphics. See how big they are there before spending a lot of time reducing their size.

Tip 79: Resizing Graphics

Warning 24: If you resize an image, it may look fine in Lectora but when published to HTML it may look grainy or pixelated. It is better to resize images in the source tool (PhotoShop, PowerPoint®, etc.).

While you can resize graphics, you will get better quality images if you adjust their size with the tool that created them or one designed to work with images. The image quality usually (not always) stays good when you make the graphic smaller. Making it larger can make the image pixilated.

This applies to the sizing tools at the bottom of the Lectora window.

Get it the right size *before* you insert into Lectora. The screen ruler is a big help here.

http://delphi.about.com/library/weekly/aa080205a.htm

Tip 80: Resize Images Proportionally

To enlarge or minimize your image proportionally, hold down your Shift key and grab the corner of the image, and drag.

Thanks to Trivantis Newsletter

Tip 81: How to See Graphic Sizes Before Inserting into Lectora

Frequently it is useful to know the dimensions of images before putting them into Lectora.

1. Open your images folder and select the View menu or ribbon and then Details.

2. Right click in the column headings and scroll down to the bottom and click on More.

3. Then check the Dimensions option.

4. A new Dimensions column will appear. You can drag it over next to your image names as shown below.

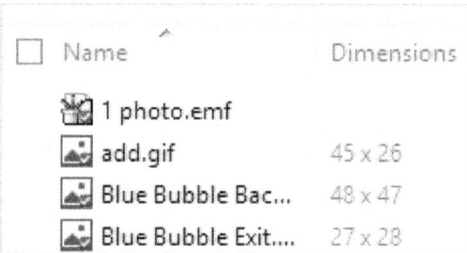

Tip 82: Reuse the Same Graphics

Warning 25: If you continually copy and paste directly from a drawing tool, Lectora creates a *new* image each time you paste. For example, if you used the same PowerPoint® diagram on three different pages, copying each time from PowerPoint® and just pasting into Lectora, Lectora now has three *different* images in the images folder. If you decide to change the diagram, you have to go to all three places to change it.

If you are inserting graphics from a Windows® folder or from the Lectora Library, Lectora will *not* create a new image file but instead will just make a new instance of an the existing one because it sees that the file name is the same. This keeps your image folder a reasonable size and can speed up how fast the page is displayed in HTML.

Therefore, a better practice is if the object already exists somewhere in the course, copy it from there to each place you use it. Then Lectora will be sure to use the same file. Now the Resource Manager can help you find all places it is used if you ever need to know.

Tip 83: Changing an Image

You can also swap it out for a new image fairly easily.

1. First, find one of the places it is used and click on it. From the Properties ribbon, get the image file name. This is the name you will see in the images folder in Windows®. In our example, this is Image 2001.bmp

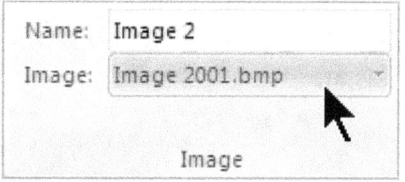

2. Paste in your new image and get its file name. Suppose that was Image 2002.bmp.

3. Then go to the images folder and delete the old image (Image 2001 above).

4. Finally, in Windows®, copy the new image and rename the copy to the old name (Image 2001).

Now, when you refresh the page in Lectora, you will see the new image. You should then delete the new image you pasted in (Image 2002) as it is not needed.

If the images were different sizes, check to be sure the new one is resized correctly. Check this on at least one by making sure the width and height are the same as the original on the Position & Size ribbon.

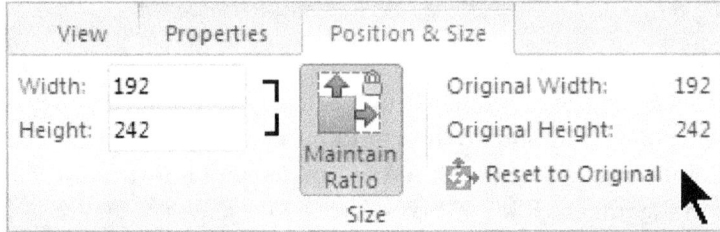

Tip 84: Best Practice on Cleaning Up Your Images Folder

Warning 26: Your images folder will sometimes have graphics left over from past work. Lectora 11 at least has no easy way of deleting unused images from the images folder. Same with video and audio file files.

1. Open Tools ribbon > Resources and click on the Unused tab and then click the Remove All button. This releases the resources from Lectora but does *not* take them out of the images folder.

2. In Lectora, File ribbon > Export > Zip.

3. Delete your old images folder, extern folder, and media folder.

4. Open the zip file, then drag and drop these folders to the folder containing your AWT file to replace the ones just deleted.

Tip 85: How to Find Where Objects Are Used

Open the Resource Manager found on the Tools ribbon.

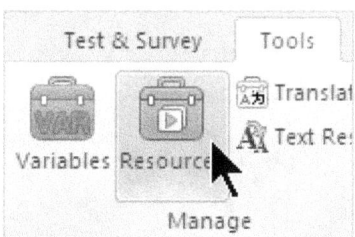

Then locate the desired object on the left in the All tab. All the locations of where the object is used are shown on the right. Just click on one to be taken there.

Tip 86: Trick for Creating Your Own Graphic Library

You don't have to save graphics as Library objects to use them quickly. Just create a folder and have it open on your desktop. Put your GIFs, JPGs, PNGs, and any other graphic objects in that folder. Then drag the graphic from there to the layout pane of your course.

D. Buttons and Menus

Buttons and menus can present their own set of challenges. Here are some tips that will make things look better and make your work go faster.

Tip 87: Making New Text Buttons with the Same Look and Feel as Others Currently in the Course

Copy the current button and paste. Then just change the text in the button.

Warning 27: Be aware that Lectora will *not* change the button file name. Say the first one was Next. Its file name in Windows® is next.gif. You copy it in Lectora and change the text to Back. But the file name is next001.gif, *not* back.gif.

If you want to change the file name, then just right click on it and select Resource Manager.

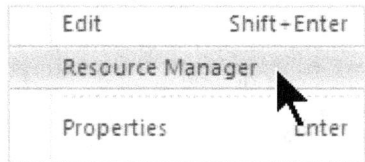

Then, in the Resource Manager, change its name and click Rename.

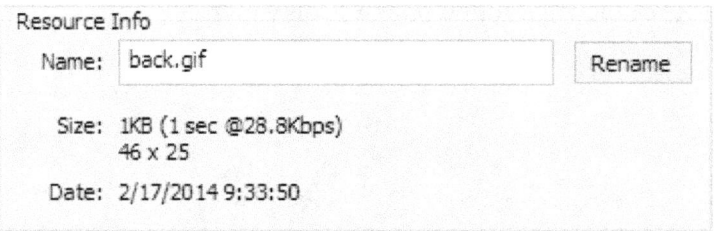

Tip 88: Resizing Buttons

If you change the font size in a button, it frequently means that the button size changes as well. You can control whether the button resizes itself by turning on "Automatically resize button to fit text" on the button Properties ribbon.

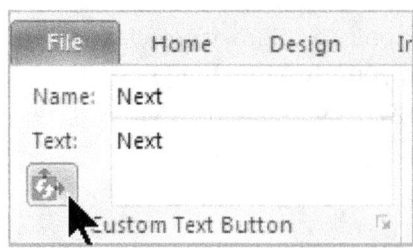

You can also control the exact size of the button using the Position & Size ribbon.

Tip 89: Select Visually Appealing Form Buttons

The default form buttons don't look very nice especially when published to HTML. Select one of the ones provided with Lectora or create your own on the Form Elements tab accessed from the File ribbon.

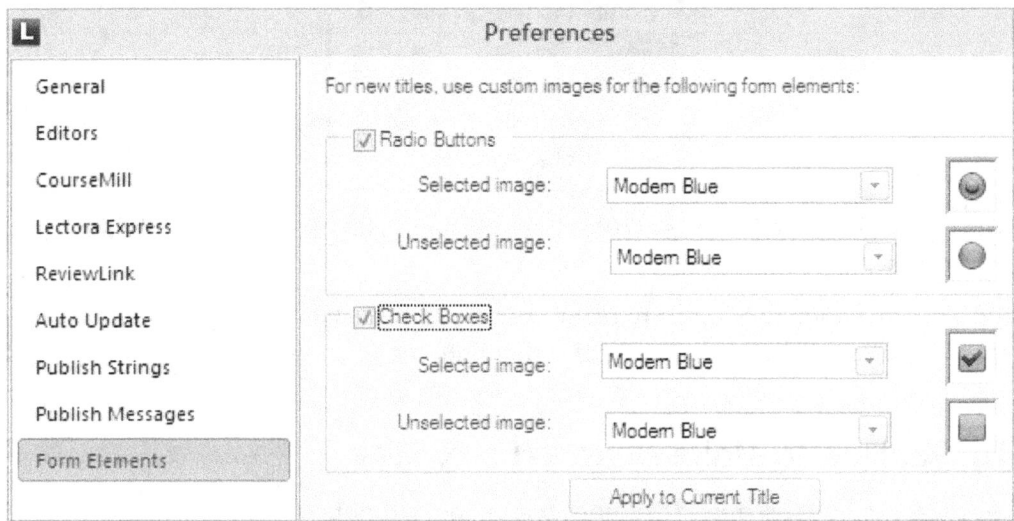

Tip 90: Select a Functional Button Color

Make buttons as familiar to the user as possible. Here are two general principles.

- Select a color that allows you to create a grayed-out state. Frequently you will need some buttons, particularly the Next button, to be grayed out (inactive). If you pick gray for your button color, you are toast! It will be very hard to create a grayed-out button.

- Select a darker color so you can create a lighter mouse-over state. This ties back to the common elevator button. When pushed, it lights up. See the next tip.

Tip 91: Use Natural Button Highlight Colors

While different colors can add interest to your buttons, in most cases it is a good idea to have the highlight color for the button in the same color family as the primary button color. The easiest way to do this is to slide the color slider in the Custom Color selector on the far right up or down.

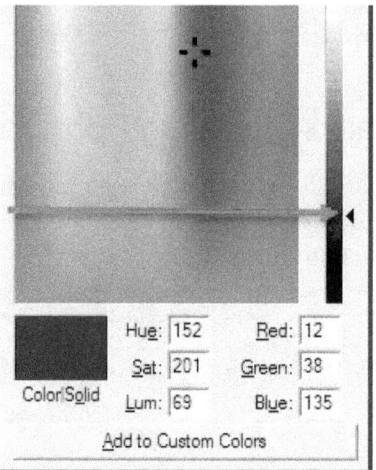

Once you have settled on a new color for your highlight, use it consistently through your course for a more professional look.

A good convention to adopt is to make the mouse-over state slightly lighter than the normal state similar to elevator buttons that light up when pressed.

Tip 92: How to Make Buttons Look Slick

Here are two buttons, one with a border and one without.

The appearance of the right button is cleaner and has a professional quality. It is easy to do. The button is 224 x 33 with a bevel height of 10. The border is a text box outline is 234 x 43, same color blue, 3px raised bevel, with a gray outline. Place it behind the button.

Tip 93: How to Access Button Parts

The buttons created by the Lectora Wizard are really three images. If you want access to one of the ones that does not show, publish the title and then look in the html/images folder for the button. You will find all three states (normal, mouse over, mouse down). You can drag and drop any one of these separate images (maybe for a grayed out version) onto your Lectora page.

Tip 94: Secrets of Floating Nav Buttons That Are at the Bottom of the Page

Some companies insist that the navigation buttons are on the bottom of the page. That works fine until you have a diagram or picture that will not fit without increasing page height just a bit. When CBTs were first introduced, people were not used to scrolling down and so this became the standard. Today scrolling is common. It is still a good idea to try to keep scrolling to a minimum but you are not as restricted as you used to be. If you want some freedom, try this.

Position the navigation buttons as desired.

Then open the Position & Size ribbon and check the Offset from Bottom box.

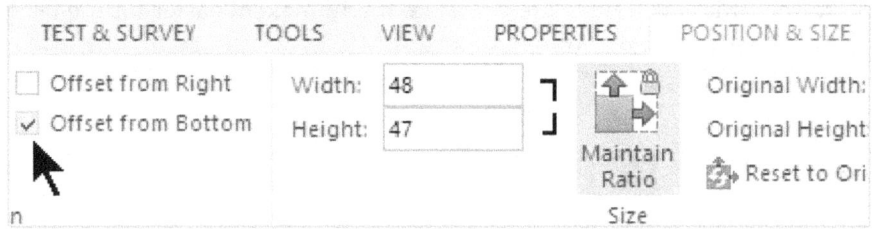

Later, if you need to make one page bigger, the navigation elements stay in place relative to the bottom of the page.

While this can be a good thing, be careful that the learner is *not* continually scrolling just to get to the Next button.

Tip 95: How to Combine a Menu with a Button

Here is a way to show and hide a menu using buttons! You may want to do this because you have a particular look and feel for your graphics buttons. Here is an example for a Help ribbon.

1. Create a regular button indicating Help.

2. Create your Help menu, make it hidden, and place it just below the button on the page.

3. Add an action to the button that says On Mouse Enter, Show your menu.

4. Add a second On Mouse Enter action to the button that hides the ribbon after 2-3 seconds.

Of course, you can make the menu show On Mouse Click instead of On Mouse Enter.

Tip 96: Using Customized Submenu Formats Effectively

While you can do anything you want with regard to the colors, here are some recommendations to keep your ribbon and submenus looking professional:

- Keep the colors in the submenu in the same family unless you have good reason. Just use the same color as the Top Level and move the slider on the far right in the custom color selector up or down.

- Make the top level (on the Menu Style tab) font one size bigger that the submenu (on the Submenu Style tab). This further emphasizes the difference between the two levels.

- Always give the background of the submenu some color *other* than the page background unless you have good reason. It will make it easier for the learner to distinguish between the two.

E. Tips when Using Groups

Groups are a powerful tool. They can make life easier, reduce the number of actions you need to use, and clean up the Title Explorer. Nevertheless, there are limitations, things you need to know that are not so obvious, and one super unpublished trick.

Tip 97: How to Have Groups within Groups

Rather than make you wait, here is the super unpublished trick. You probably know that Lectora does not support nested Groups – Groups within Groups. But, it seems that you can put Forms in groups. And, Forms can contain objects other than Form objects (radio buttons, check boxes, etc.). Doing it the right way, you can put text blocks and images inside forms. Then, effectively, you can have nested groups. Also, it appears that you can put Forms inside Forms this way although I have not tried it in a production course.

Here is one example for feedback. I have one action to hide all the feedback by hiding the "all feedback" group so no matter which feedback was shown last, it will be hidden. Then I have just one action to show the appropriate feedback – I show one of the Forms, which contains a text block and a graphic.

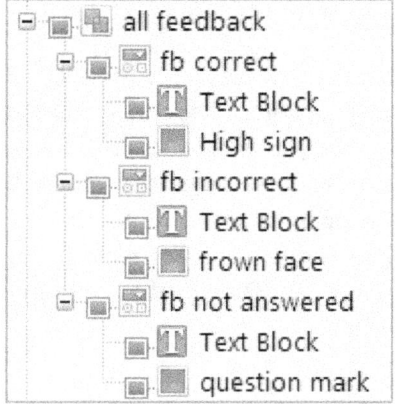

1. Create your group first.

2. Then create the Forms.

3. Then create your text blocks and drag them into the Forms.

4. Then drag anything else you want into the Forms.

Note: It appears that you have to put the text block in the form first. Then you can add graphics. Not sure why.

Tip 98: How to Move Just *One* Object in a Group

If you go to reposition just one item in a group, when you drag it, it will drag the other objects in the group. Sometimes that is a good thing. Sometimes not. Here are ways to reposition just one item.

• You can drag just one item in a group by holding the Alt key down and then clicking and dragging or moving it with the arrow keys.

• You can change the X or Y coordinate by setting them in the status bar at the bottom of the Lectora Edit window

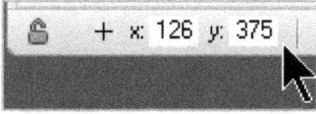

or on the or on the Position & Size ribbon

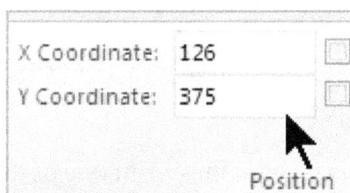

• You drag the edges of a text block which will resize it but that may be okay.

Tip 99: Good Practice for Naming Groups

Begin the group name with either "actions- " or "objects- ". Follow that with a capital letter of the rest of the name. Examples: "actions- Common feedback" and "objects- Feedback." Then in the left pane, put all the action groups together in alphabetic order and all the object groups as close together as possible based on layering with other objects. This makes it sooooo much easier to find stuff when coding actions or making changes. Here is an example from a page with a game. All the actions are together, all the objects are together. The Feedback group is last because it needed to layer on top of the other groups.

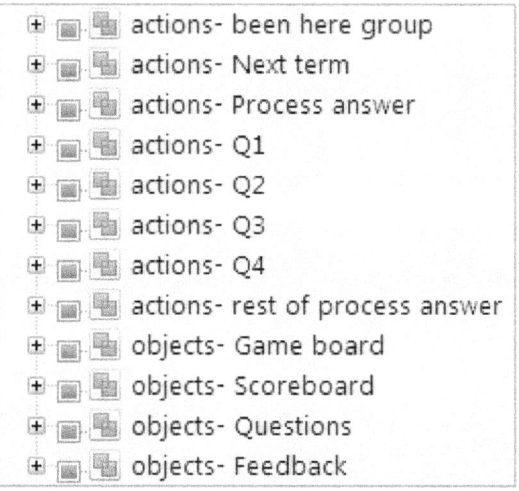

 **Warning 28:** Oh, do not use a colon (Ex. actions:) because if you ever try to save it as a Lectora Library object, it will not save but Lectora will *not* warn you! It simply does not save it. Bummer.

F. Tips for Actions and Variables

Okay, this section is for the more advanced developers. These tips will make development easier and more reliable when you are using actions and variables. They will also help you debug problems.

Tip 100: Speeding Up Selecting Objects or Variables from a Drop-down List

When you go to select objects or variables from one of the dropdown lists such as the Inherit or the Show/Hide selection window, you may frequently have to do a lot of scrolling. Even worse, you may accidently select the wrong one! **By using the following naming conventions, this work will go a lot faster with fewer mistakes.**

Naming Conventions for Objects

Begin the name of all the objects that are *inherited* from the title, chapter, or section level with a letter at the *end* of the alphabet. This way, when you click on a drop-down list to select an object as in a Show action or changing which objects are inherited, all the *inherited* objects are together and at the *bottom* – out of the way. All the objects on the page are together at the top of the list and all the inherited objects (that you are less likely to want to hide or show) are at the bottom of the list.

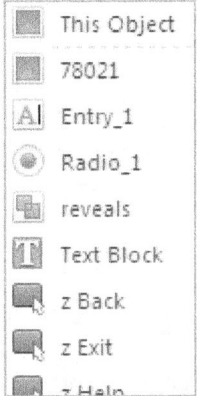

- Begin title and AU level objects with **z** – ex. z Next
- Begin chapter level objects with **y** – y Chapter icon
- Begin section level objects with **x** – x Section title

Other Useful Naming Conventions

Suppose you have three buttons on the screen that are to be clicked or moused over by the learner to show more information. Each button Shows and Hides different text blocks and pictures. I code everything with similar names but differentiate by prefixing or appending a 1, 2, or 3 to each object. That way I can create the actions for the first set and then copy and paste them to the other buttons. Then just change the targets, which will be readily locatable when opening the Target property. Example:

- Photo 1
- Photo 2
- Photo 3

In big courses, I find it useful to include some kind of key word in the graphic name when it is being created in an external graphic tool.

- Include "diag" in diagram names
- Include "photo" in photograph names

- etc.

Then, when you need to find where diagrams or photos are used, you can open the Resource Manager, click on the appropriate category, click the Search tab and enter the key word.

Use This Naming Convention for Variables

Make the first character in all user created variables an underscore (_your_variable).

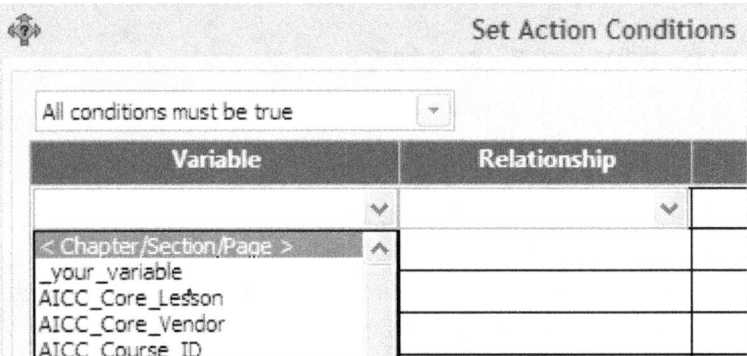

Why? Because it separates all your variables from all the Lectora reserved variables and it brings *your variables to the top in the variable list.* This makes it easier to find when selecting variables for Conditions or other uses.

Notice here that *your_variable* is listed first even though the first letter is a v.

Tip 101: Best Practice Naming Pages

Warning 29: Don't name your Lectora pages using a period. A community forum member named one "offensive lang." and it messed up the coding later causing the LMS unable to display that page. Why, you ask? It ended up causing two periods side by side (..) in the source coding.

So, if you are having this problem you might look to see if you named a page using a period in the name. After you fix and republish, be sure to refresh when you get to that page in the LMS.

Thanks to Kelechim.

It is probably a good idea *not* to use any other Windows special characters /*?:<>|''' either.

Tip 102: Speed Up Creating Actions That Reference Popup Pages

During development, drag your popup chapter to the beginning of the course (the top of the list in the Title Explorer). This way, when you are creating actions to display these pages, they will appear at the beginning of the list instead of the end.

Then, when you are finished developing, drag it back to the end.

During Development

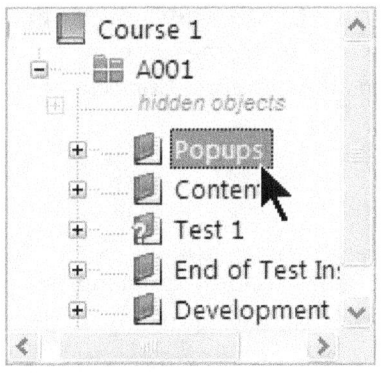

After Development

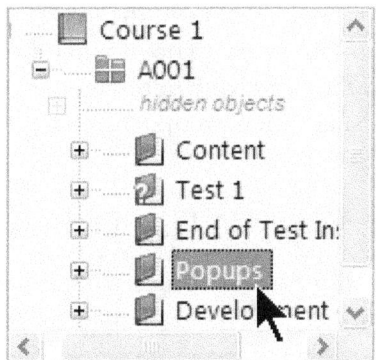

Tip 103: Easy Ways to Repeat the Same Conditions on Multiple Actions

When you have several actions with the same conditions, there are several ways you can make your life easier. These are useful, not just the first time, but also later on when you may have to change the conditions.

- Group Actions with Similar Conditions

Create a group and put all the actions you want to run at the same time under the same conditions in the group. Then, on the action that runs the group put all the conditions on that action. **If things change, you only need to change that <u>one</u> action.**

- Copy and Paste the Conditions

Create the conditions on the first action. Click the **Copy Conditions** button at the bottom of the conditions window. Note that this does *not* use the clipboard so whatever you have in it is undisturbed.

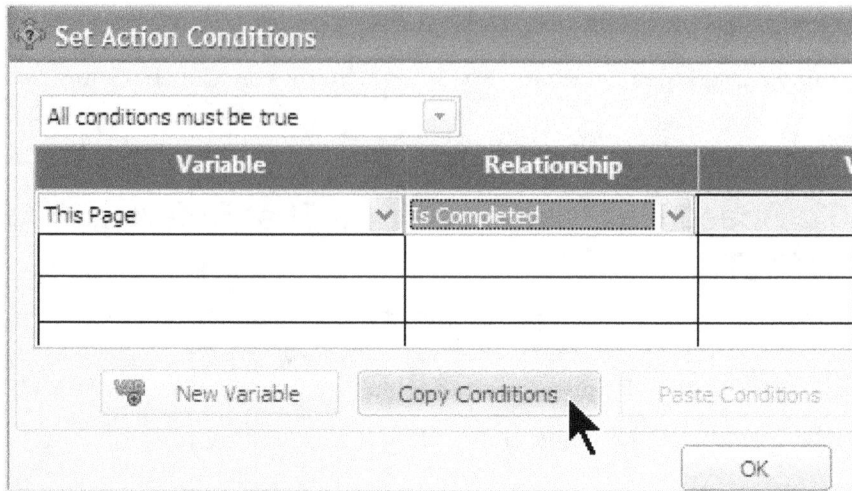

Then in the actions that need the same conditions, click the **Paste Conditions** button. While this is fairly easy to do, if you have several actions all using the same conditions, they you have to remember to change them all when conditions change. Consider using action groups instead.

Tip 104: When to Use Debug Mode

When you start having trouble with actions not working or variables not being set correctly, first publish your course and remove any errors. Run and Preview mode will not show theses

Then use one of these debug feature. You can see actions firing, the value of variables, and even change the values.

Debug Mode from Lectora

On the View ribbon, click Debug.

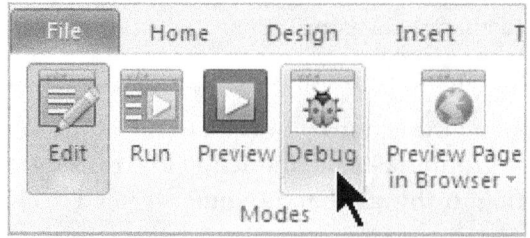

If you use it a lot, put it on the Quick Access Toolbar. Note that it is listed as Run in Debug Mode, not just Debug Mode.

Debug Mode when Published

When published, you need to check the debug option in the Publish Options.

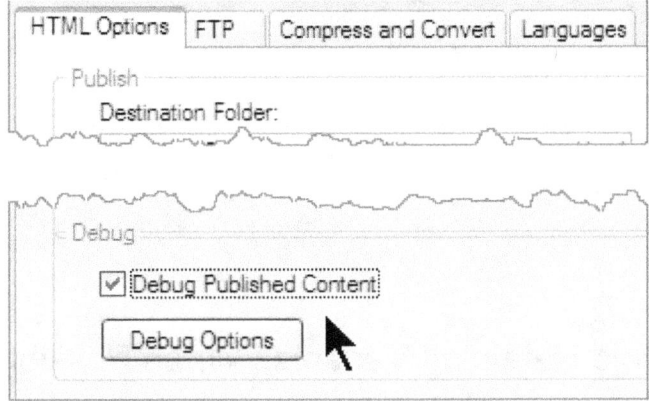

Tip 105: Finding Actions You Are Looking for in the Debug Window

To make a desired action stand out in the debug window, just a string of =============== to the end of an action name.

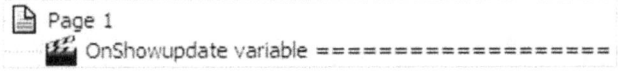

Tip 106: How to Find Where You Used Variables

As soon as you start having trouble with variables used across pages, go to the variable manager and make sure that you have not used them elsewhere. Access the variable manager from the Tools ribbon.

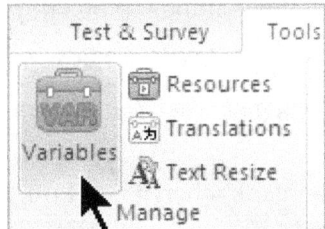

Then you can just click on any line it shows and your layout pane will move to that page and action. There you can see the actions using the variable.

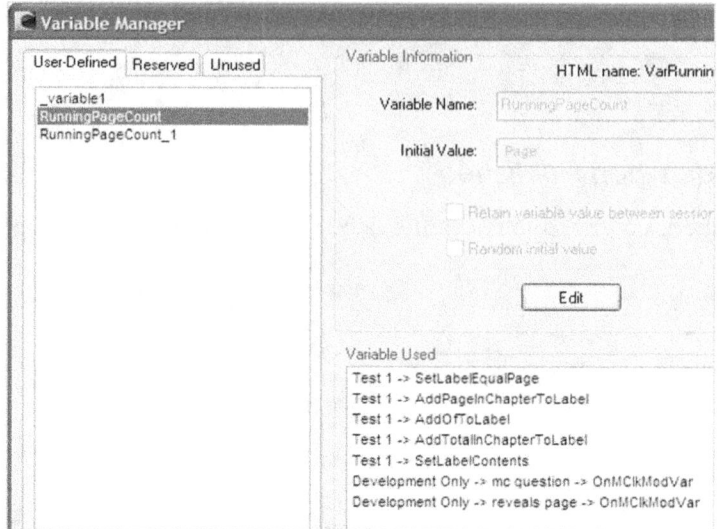

Tip 107: Avoid Retaining Variables When Possible

Warning 30: While it is a nice idea, retaining variable values between sessions can cause problems. Most LMSs have a limit of 4K. If you start retaining all your variables, you could exceed that limit and cause unpredictable behavior when the course is launched the second time. See Coping with Storage Limits on page 102.

G. Popup Window Tips

There are many ways to create a popup window. Some are real new Windows, some are just showing something on the current page.

Tip 108: Controlling Popup Window Names

The name that appears in the banner at the top of a popup window is:

- The *course name* when the window is a Light Box

- The *page name* of the popup page in the Title Explorer when it is displayed as a New Window in HTML

- Either "Popup Window" or blank when using Run, Preview, or Published to Executable.

Tip 109: Certificate Wizard Tip

Certificates are frequently put in popup Windows and Lectora has a nice collection of a dozen different designs. If you do not like any of the 12 choices, get one you like somewhat and tweak it. Find out the size of the background graphic and create one of your own the same size and replace. This is probably a lot better than starting from ground zero.

Also, if you don't like the date format, check out the Date Formatting and Calculating add-on available from the www.eProficiency.com/webStore.

H. Power Tips for Tests and Questions

This section gives you tips on setting up tests and questions. The tips on questions apply to questions inside as well as outside of a Test.

These are some tips designed to do different things related to the learner doing things you don't want them to. They reduce the exposure of the correct answers in a Test as well as protect your content.

Good Design Practices

Tip 110: Use Familiar Navigation

When you create a Test, Lectora automatically creates buttons and page numbering. Rather than suddenly introducing new navigation buttons to the learner, delete all this and simply inherit the buttons used in the rest of the course.

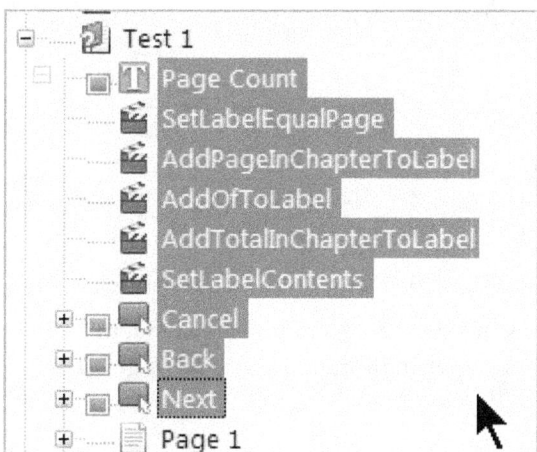

Tip 111: Set the Proper Test Properties

Click on the Test Chapter icon in the Title Explorer.

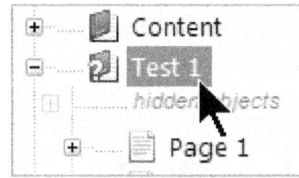

Now you have access to the Behavior and the Results properties for the Test.

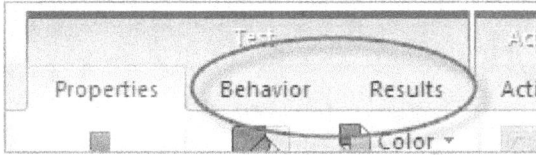

Behavior Ribbon

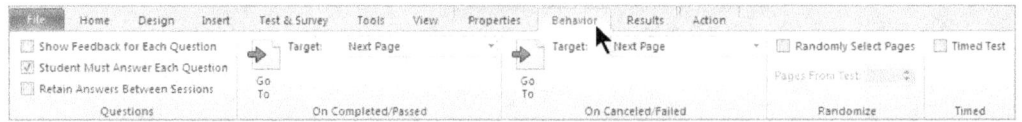

Set the desired options. If you want to retain the answers to all questions, be sure to read the section on Coping with Storage Limits on page 102.

When Completed/Passed and When Canceled/Failed Tab

Warning 31: If you have no pages after your Test (no popup chapter, no development chapter, no nothing), then scored Tests will work in Run mode but *not* when published to HTML.

For clarity and ease of development, create a separate chapter after each of your Tests containing a Passed and a Failed page. Each page gives explains to the learner how they fared on the Test and what they should do next.

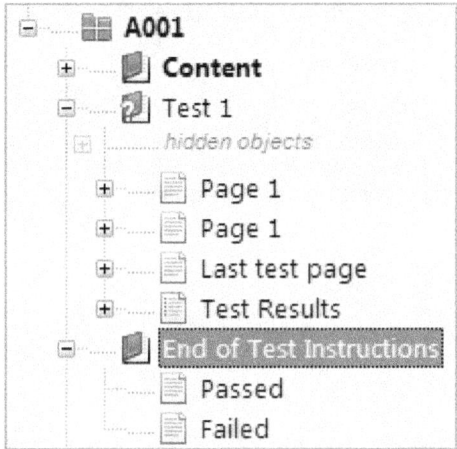

Then on the Test Behavior ribbon, specify which page the Test should go to in the When Completed/Passed and When Canceled/Failed areas when the Test is scored (Submitted/Processed).

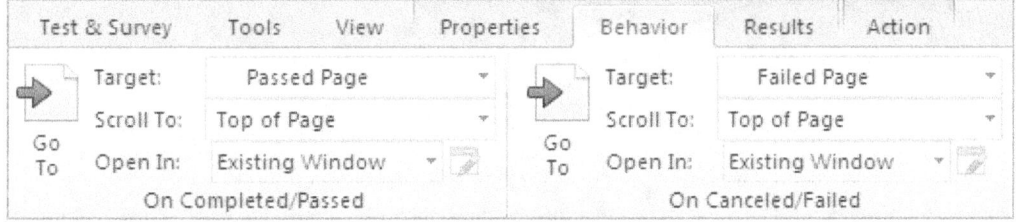

Results Ribbon

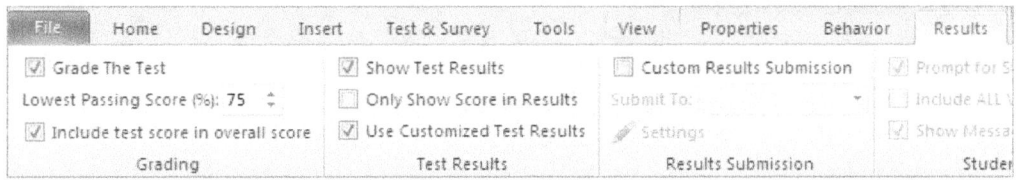

Check the desired boxes.

If you want the student to see detailed question-by-question results, you have two choices: a default Results page or a Customized Test Results page.

1. If you just check Show Test Results, then the student will receive a standard popup window at the end of the Test before going to the Passed or Failed page.

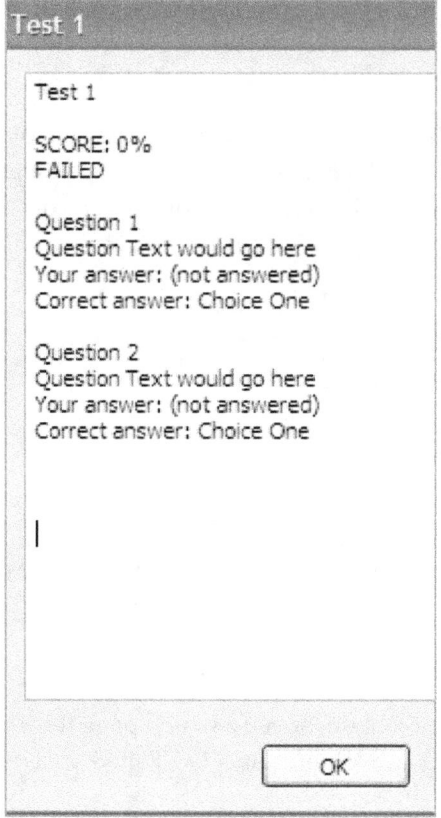

2. If you check that and the Customized Test Results,

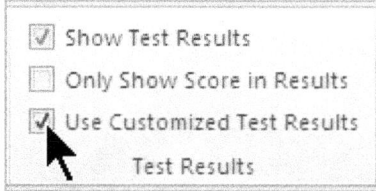

then you will see a new *red* page added at the end of the Test.

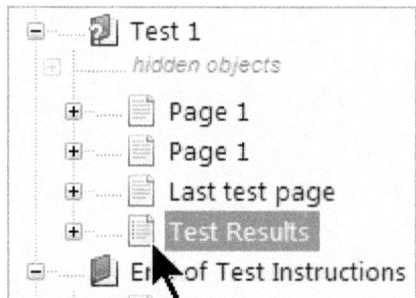

When you click on it, you will see a new ribbon, Content.

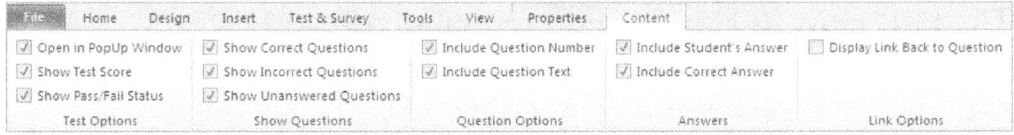

Here you have many options you can select from.

Tip 112: Fix the Last Page for Non-randomized Tests

If you have a Test, then you need to have it scored. For a *non-randomized* Test, you need an action like this somewhere on the last page of the Test. One way to do this is to replace the Next button with one that has this action.

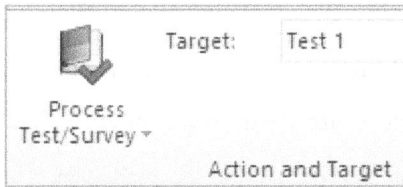

Nothing is needed for a randomized Test.

Tips for Questions and Feedback

Tip 113: Good Practice Naming Questions

Sometimes I find it useful to change the variable name if it is referenced in another part of the course. This usually happens *not* in a Test but rather when using questions in regular content chapters in exercises. Then I adopt the convention of copying the name of the variable and pasting it into the name of the question so I don't have to open it up to get the variable name. The names of the variables are right there in the Title Manage pane when I go to create actions that use the variables.

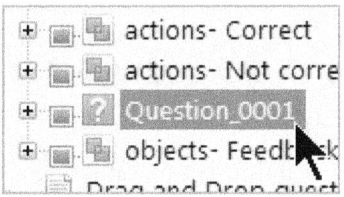

Warning 32: One caution is that if you copy the questions into another part of the title or another title, the question numbers are likely to change but the names of the questions in the Title Explorer will not. You will have to manually go in and change those names yourself.

Tip 114: How to Easily Align Question Objects

Align the Entire Question with Something Else on the Page

If you want to move the entire question, click on the question icon in the Title Explorer to select the entire question (all the choices, boxes/buttons, and the question text, and any images). You can drag this anywhere.

Align Objects within the Question <u>Only</u>

If you want to move one or two objects within the question, begin by clicking in an unused portion of the page to deselect the question. Then you have several alternatives:

1. Click on each one you want on the page while holding the Ctrl key down OR

2. Click on each one you want in the left pane while holding the Ctrl key down OR

3. Click and hold in an unused portion of the page and drag over the objects you want to select.

Then click any of the alignment icons (top, bottom, left, right, space, or center)

Align Some Question Objects with Objects <u>Outside</u> the Question

Okay, now it's harder. Lectora does not seem to let you select objects from within and objects outside the question using alternatives 1 and 2 above. However, alternative 3 (click and drag to select) *does* work.

By the way, this same technique also works for aligning objects inside and outside a group or at different levels (title, chapter, page).

Tip 115: How to Give One Feedback for Several Questions on a Single Page

Sometimes you may have several fill-in-the-blank questions on a single page. The learner perceives this as one question. Don't use the feedback built in to the Question Wizard, as it is difficult to get the kind of feedback you want.

1. Have one button that says "Check My Answer".

2. Use the condition tab on an action to check all question variables on the page for "correct". If not, show a text block with the incorrect feedback. If one question is unanswered, it is incorrect.

Tip 116: How to Change the Font in a Drop List or Fill-in-the-Blank Question

When using the drop list or a FIB question for teaching software, you may need to have a different font than is shown in the drop list box. The page font controls that font.

1. Uncheck the Inherit box on the page properties.

2. Change the default font for that page and then change the text boxes for instructions back to the regular text on the screen using a Style.

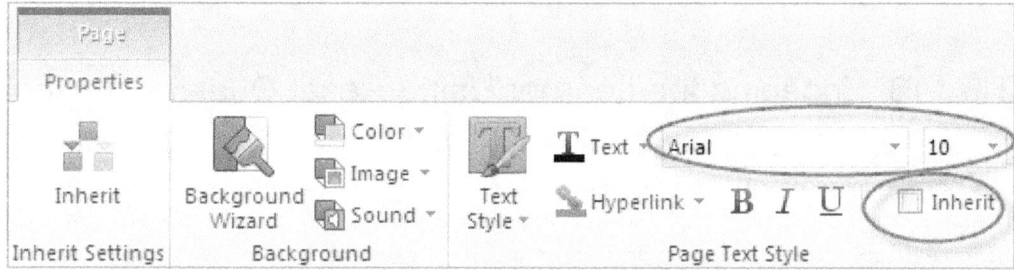

Tip 117: Why You Should Avoid Matching Questions

The whole idea behind asking questions is to help the learner remember the material. While matching questions sound nice and are quite common, they do *not* help the learner remember the material. The answer is a bunch of crisscrossed lines connecting things. If you can, it is much better to *use a drag and drop question* so that when done, the page is something that you want the learner to remember.

I mean, how memorable is this?

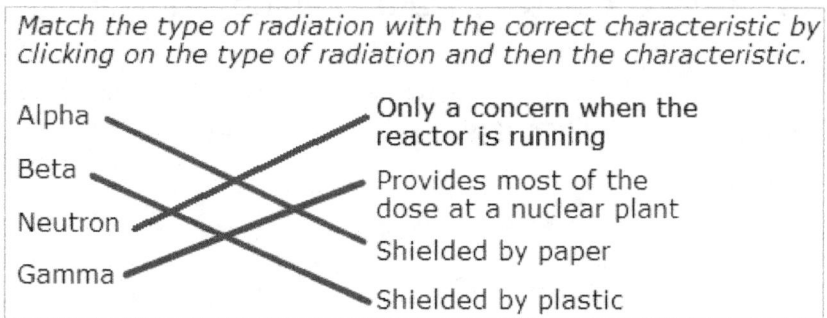

Compare that to changing this to a drag and drop question shown next.

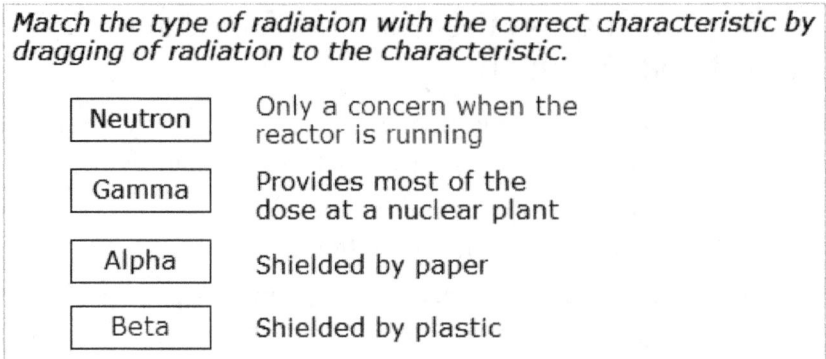

Tip 118: Engaging the Learner Using Reset Question Action

Another way to engage the learner is to allow them to try the question again by clearing everything. Adults frequently like to try things (we learn most things by trial and error). Use the Reset action for more than just the multiple-choice questions. Add matching and drag and drop and the Reset action to allow them to try again with a clean slate.

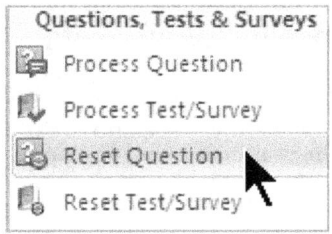

Tip 119: Partial Credit (Separate Grading) Caution

Warning 33: Using partial credit (checking the Grade each choice box) to allow the student to get some credit can lead to very confusing scoring.

While this is another great sounding feature, it can throw you off balance concerning grading. Say you build a Test with 10 questions, one of which uses has four choices with Grade each choice checked. What you really have is *thirteen* questions, not *ten* – nine regular questions plus the four choices from the separate grading question. Try explaining that to the learner when they get a low score!

Ways to Reduce Cheating

Tip 120: Create Questions with a Twist

Put the question text and choices text outside the question wizard in a separate text box. Then, in the question wizard only use A, B, C, D ... Then the XML becomes much less usable.

Tip 121: Make It Harder to Copy Answers (Part 1)

Begin with this cool option when you publish.

Tip 122: Make It Harder to Copy Answers (Part 2)

As an alternative, you can randomize the sequence the answer choices appear for Multiple-choice and Multiple Response questions. Just check the Randomize choices box on the Question tab of the question properties.

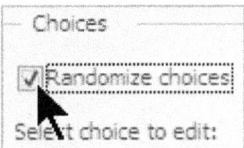

If it is an existing question, you will have to click the Edit Question button on the question Properties ribbon first.

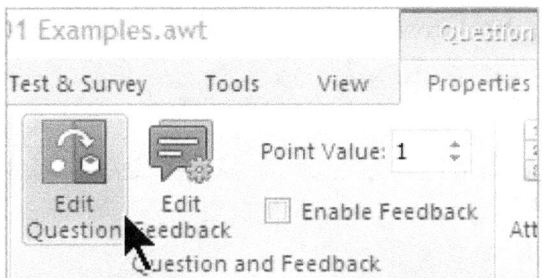

Tip 123: Make It Harder to Copy Answers (Part 3)

Randomize the sequence in which the questions are shown to the learner by checking the Randomly Select Pages box on the Behavior ribbon for a Test chapter

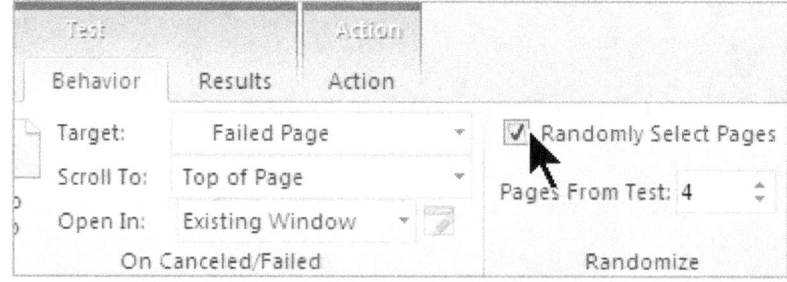

or on the Behavior ribbon of a Test Section.

Tip 124: How to Disable Native Browser Navigation Keys

Include actions at the title level that display a warning message for the following keys:

- Alt+Left Arrow

- Backspace

- Ctrl-P (so they can't print the page)

- PrintScreen and Ctrl-PrintScreen

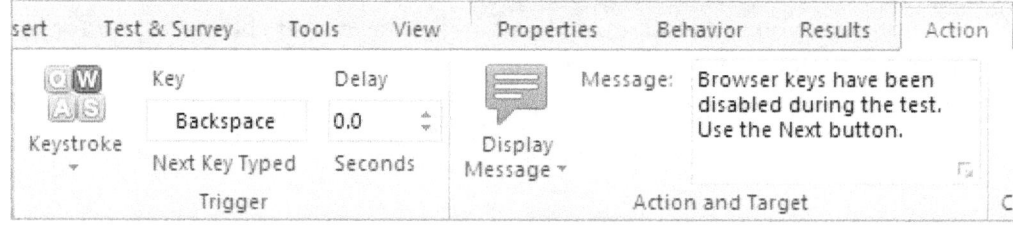

Tip 125: How to Disable Right Mouse Click, Double Clicking, and Dragging

1. Create an HTML object from the Insert ribbon.

2. Then select: Object Type: Other

3. Insert:

   ```
   <body oncontextmenu="return false" onselectstart="return false" ondrag-
   start="return false">
   ```

in the Custom HTML field.

Thanks to JohnfromLondon and others

Tip 126: How to Disable the Browser Back Button

When someone clicks the IE back button, this code prevents the page from showing and returns immediately to the page where the back button was clicked.

1. Click the "HTML Extension" button on the Insert ribbon.

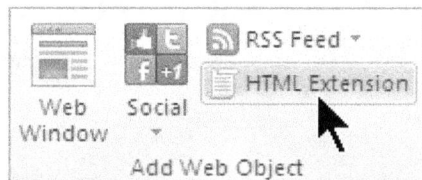

2. Click the Type arrow on its Properties ribbon and select "Meta tags."

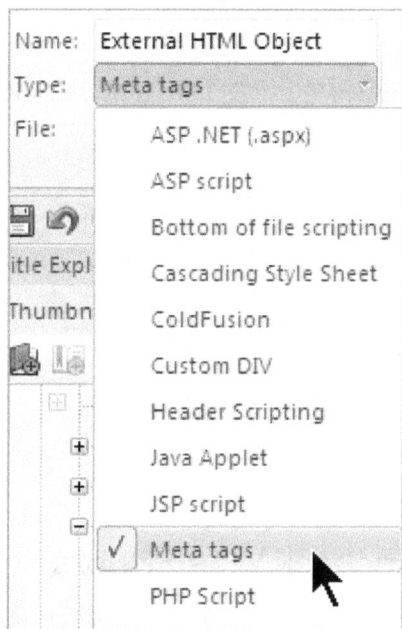

3. Click the Edit button on the Properties ribbon.

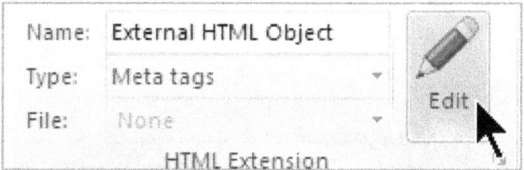

4. In the HTML extension box that opens, enter the following code:

```
<script>history.forward();</script>
```

Thanks to Lex_Tensions

Tip 127: How to Prevent User from Changing Answers

The easiest way now with Lectora 11 is to go to the Attempts tab in a question and set it to 1.

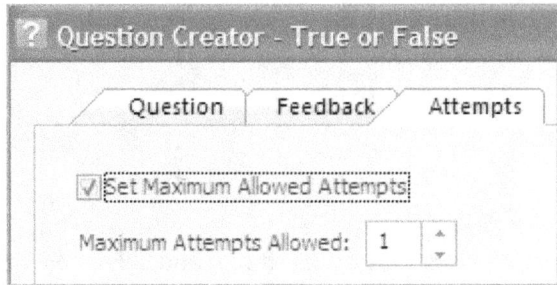

Tip 128: How to Prevent Reading Feedback Using View Source

If you are showing hidden text boxes for your feedback, then all someone has to do is View Source and they can see the feedback. To hide it and make it harder to find the answer, just check the Convert To Image property for the feedback text box.

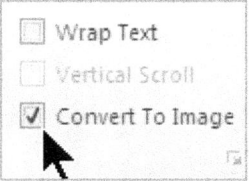

Tip 129: What to Uncheck When Publishing

For additional security, when publishing, *uncheck* the option to use the JavaScript Title Explorer. The content will now use Java and the Test file will be a .bin file, which is binary. Be sure to test the published file on target machines as not all have the appropriate Java Runtime installed.

Thanks to Aaron of Trivantis

I. Tips for Miscellaneous Objects

And a few tips that just don't want to play well with the other tips so I had to put them in a room by themselves.

Tip 130: Setting PDF Display Properties

To do this, you need to first have Adobe Professional or later. (9.0 does this.)

1. Open your document with Adobe Professional, then click File > Properties.

2. Under the document properties, click the tab, "Initial View."

3. You will see three options: Layout and Magnification, Window Options, and User Interface Options.

4. Under **Layout and Magnification**: Change the Page Layout to "Single Page" and for Magnification change to "Fit Page" or "100%."

5. Under **Window Options**, check the box, "Open in Full Screen mode."

6. As you see, you could choose other options. I would make the above changes, test, and modify until you get the Initial View that is right for you.

7. **Save** the file to a new name and then test in Lectora.

Thanks to Bruman

Tip 131: Controlling Tab Order

The sequence in which objects appear in the left pane from top to bottom controls the tab order for entry fields. To some extent, tab order for entry fields can be controlled with a one-line JavaScript action. When you want to make it so that the cursor is in a specific entry field, you need to make it have the current focus. To do that, first open the properties of the entry field and click on the diagonal in the corner of the name area.

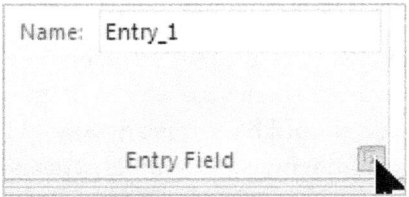

This will open a description entry area and at the bottom is the HTML name.

Then create an action that looks generally like this:

#	Trigger	Action	Target
1	Page Show	Run JavaScript	document.HTMLnameform.EntryName.focus()

For example, if the HTMLname = entry37 and the Entry name was Entry_1, then the value property would look like this:

> document.entry37form.Entry_1.focus()

Note: This worked fine in IE8 but I have not been able to get it to work in IE11.

Tip 132: How to Get a the Progress Bar to Restart for Each Chapter

Currently if you want page numbering to *restart* from one for each chapter, all you have to do is change the variables used from PageInTitle to PageInChapter and from PagesInTitle to PagesInChapter. The Progress Bar is not as easy. One way to achieve this is to put a separate Progress Bar in each chapter.

Another way is to create a Custom Progress Bar with a scale of 0-100. Then calculate the percent of the chapter complete using the PageInChapter and PagesInChapter variables and using that to set the Progress Bar. Attach these actions to the Progress Bar.

#	Trigger	Action	Target	Type	Value
1	Page Show	Modify Variable	_temp	Set Equal	VAR(PageInChapter)
2	Page Show	Modify Variable	_temp	Divide	VAR(PagesInChapter)
3	Page Show	Modify Variable	_temp	Multiply	100
4	Page Show	Set Progress Bar Position	Progress Bar		VAR(_temp)

Tip 133: When Was the Course Published?

I have seen this come up over and over again. Someone asks which version of the course this is or when was it published. One way to do this is fairly easy. Create an About This Course page (you should have this anyway) with a one-line description of the course, the authors, and the revision number. This is a good start but many times the revision number does not get changed when it should. Add a text block that displays the Published Date using the Lectora reserved variable. Add this action to the text block:

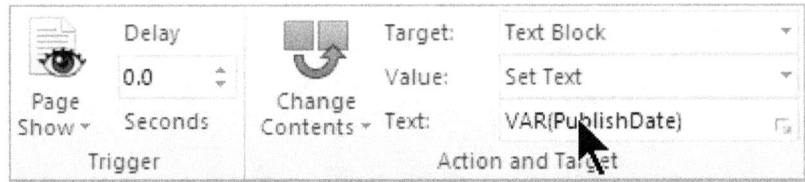

You can also put "Published: VAR(PublishDate)" in the Text field and make it easier to set up.

J. Your Notes

When you find things that will give you more power, make a note of them here.

3. Reviewing, Publishing, and Testing Tips

Now that you have your course developed, you might think you are done. But, of course, that is not the case. That would be too easy.

Here are a few tips to speed up your publishing, testing, and the review process.

A. Publishing & Testing Considerations

We begin with some general tips that don't seem to fit into the other groups regarding publishing and testing your course. My recommendation is that you apply these first before moving on to the other groups.

Tip 134: Fix Your Errors

Warning 34: You may have errors that do *not* show when you try your course in Run or Preview modes. These errors *only* show when you Publish your course.

When you do publish, you must fix any red error. Simply double-click on the error and you will be taken to the offending part of your course.

You should also minimize the number of blue warnings by fixing them because sometimes there are some that could affect your course.

Tip 135: Navigating to Any Page Quickly During Testing

When testing your course, it sometimes takes lots of time to step through all the pages and it really is not always necessary, especially when you have a few pages deep in the course you need to check out. To get around this, create a dropdown Table of Contents and place it at the top of the page. Make it always on top. Then delete it before you publish your production version.

Tip 136: Two Ways to Repeatedly Launch a Published Course

If you are repeatedly opening a course for testing, here are a few quick ideas on how to launch the course more quickly.

- The first time the course is launched, change the browser Home Page under Internet Options to be the current page or
- Create shortcut to the desired page by simply dragging the URL from the address window of the browser to your desktop or a folder.

Then you can easily launch the course repeatedly without having to hunt around for the index.html page.

Tip 137: How to Speed Up Publishing

Sometimes you are working on one page and it is giving you problems when published. Of course, at those times, you are working on a long title, the page is near the end, and the Preview in Browser button does not work for any number of reasons. Next time you have this problem, try this. It works for some situations.

Drag the page(s) you are testing to near the front of the title. Then, when published, they are updated first. You can click on the index.html page in the html folder and start looking at the page long before publishing has finished. (See previous tip for easily launching the course.) You can also simply leave the browser window open and click the refresh icon, which is frequently some kind of partial circle with an arrow.

Tip 138: Speeding up Publishing with Lots of Audio of Video

When you select one of the compression options, Lectora compresses audio, video, and images *every* time you publish.

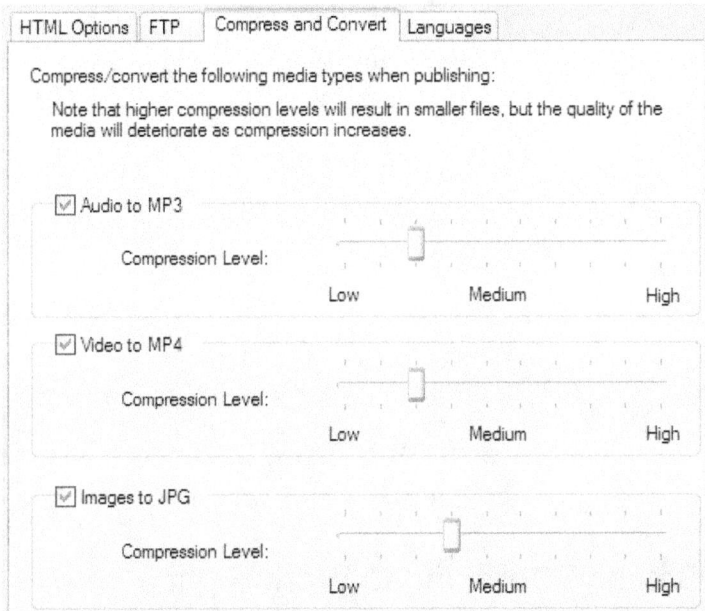

This may cause your publishing process to take a long time (like 5-10 minutes). Most courses should publish in under a minute. If yours takes longer than that, see if it is compressing any objects (watch the publishing messages). If so, make note of them. Then locate these resources in the Resource Manager and compress them once there by clicking on them and clicking the Convert to MP4/MP3 button. This can greatly speed up publishing.

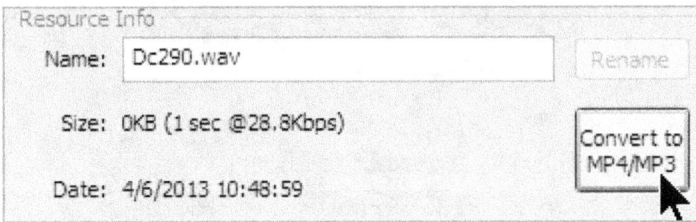

Usually these are WAV or WMV files. You can find them easily in the Resource Manager by clicking the Search tab and entering .wav or .wmv in the search box.

You can also just right click on them in the layout area and select Convert to MP3.

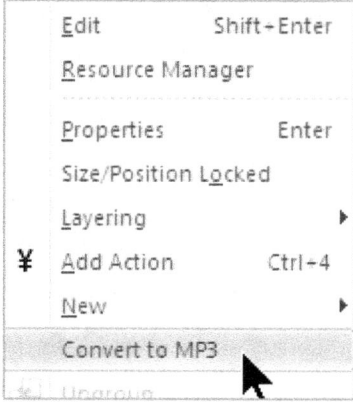

Tip 139: Getting Publishing to Work Right

Warning 35: I have seen the publish option "Publish Only Updated Pages/Resources" *not* publish pages where only the actions had been changed.

When you are tweaking only *actions* on a page or inherited objects or actions, it is better to publish all pages. Be sure this option is selected when you publish.

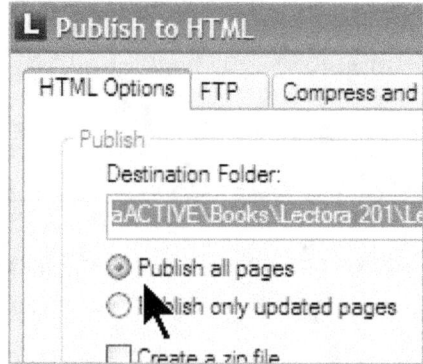

Tip 140: High-speed Find and Replace

You can use the translation tool to save time when you have many "find and re-place" changes to make to a course. It is a quicker method than using the Lectora Find and Replace, especially when you have several of these to do. Export the text with the translation tool as described above, make the changes using **WordPad**, and then Import.

Warning 36: As I said before, the Translation Tool is a powerful and potentially dangerous technique. Be sure to read the chapter on Tips for Using the Translations Tool later in this book to avoid all the pitfalls.

Tip 141: Popup Blocker

Here is how to turn off that annoying message that may show up in IE even if you have turned the popup blocker off.

- In IE 10, you can click on the gear on the right and select Internet options.

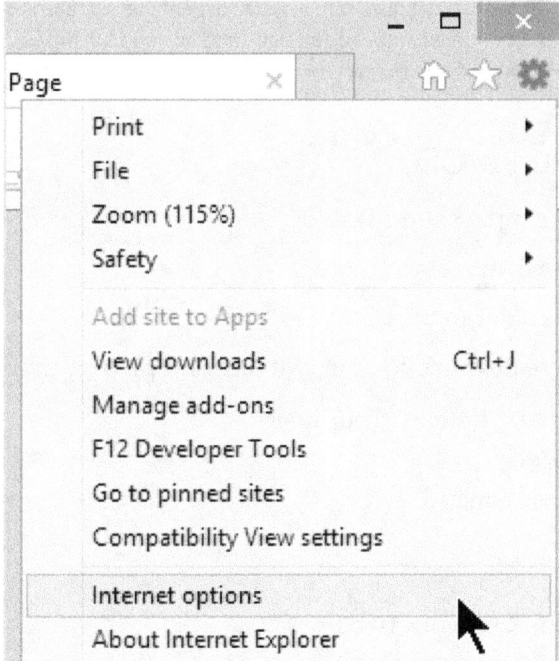

- Or you Access the Tools menu by either pressing the Alt key or right clicking on some part of the top banner and selecting it and then Internet options from there.

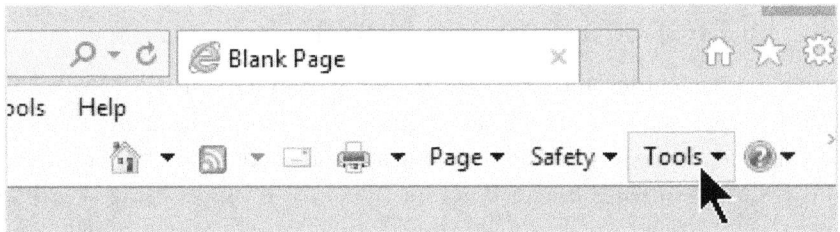

- Then click the Advanced tab > Security section and check Allow active content to run.

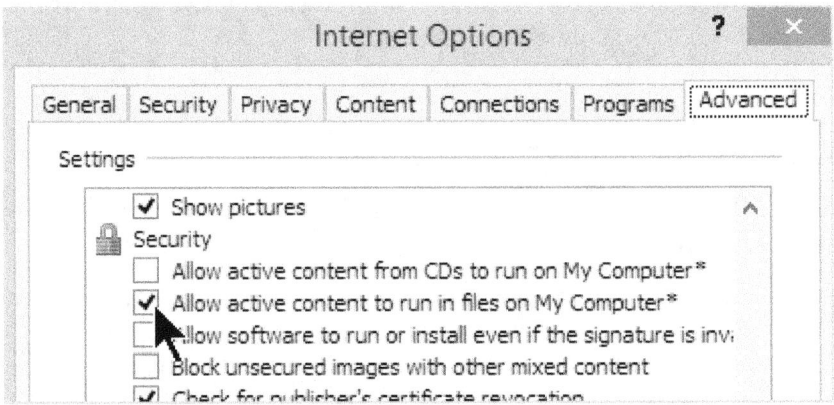

Tip 142: Autorun a CD

Try this with a very simple course first.

1. Publish your HTML as usual.

1. Copy the HTML folder to the CD.

2. Using Notepad create the following two files and place them on the CD:

Filename= autorun.bat. Contents= four lines:

```
@echo Loading CD
@start html/index.html
@cls
@exit
```

Filename=autorun.inf. Contents=two lines:

```
[autorun]
open=autorun.bat
```

Some things are not so obvious when you publish and test your course. These tips help you speed up publishing which should take less than a minute for 50 page courses and give you some things you should know about target browsers.

Tip 143: What You Should Know about Publishing and Page Names

When Lectora publishes to HTML, it creates page names that include the chapter name and the section name. This can cause problems when run over the internet because the URL is too long. It is generally a good idea when publishing the final version to HTML to turn on the Convert page names to short ID-based names option.

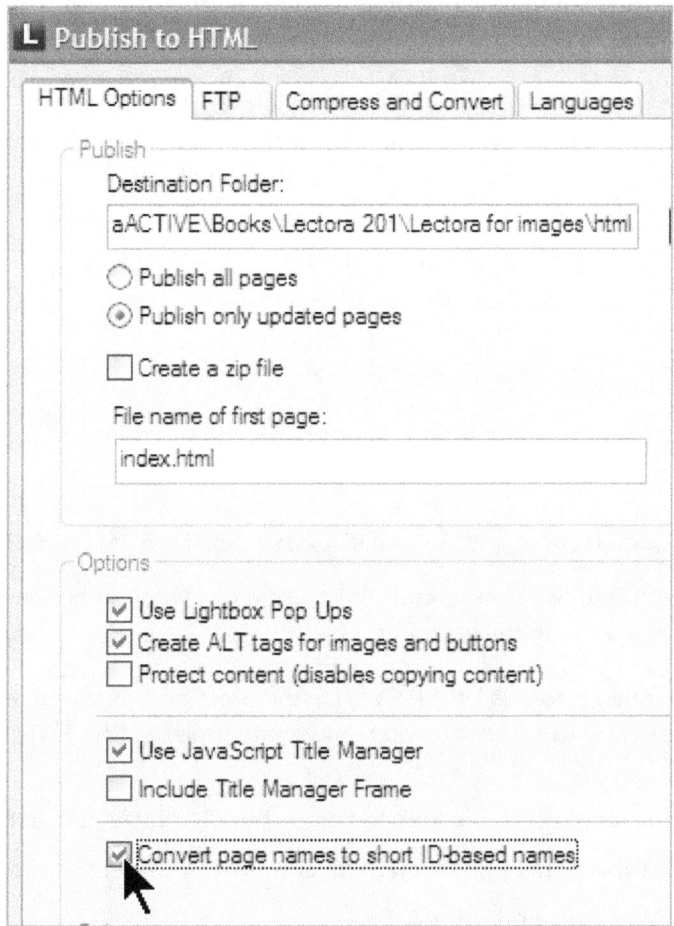

Selecting this option also allows you to use special characters in your page names although I do not advise using them.

Tip 144: Publishing Settings for a Mac

To get actions with conditions to work on a Mac, make these settings when you publish:

- Turn off "Web 2.0 Popup Window",

- turn on "Include Title Explorer Window",

- and "JavaScript Title Explorer" when publishing. Thanks so much for your help.

  Thanks to Duane Sell

Tip 145: Will They Zoom or Not?

Warning 37: Things can look a lot different to the learner depending on the browser zoom setting. Don't take chances. View your course with different zoom settings.

In earlier versions of Lectora combined with earlier versions of IE, there could be problems. After some testing, I can no longer find any differences so either Lectora 11 or Microsoft® has fixed the problems.

Still, you should advise learners to view your course with the browser zoom factor set to 100% in IE. Not sure about the other browsers.

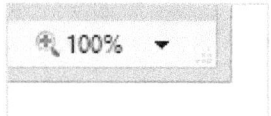

Tip 146: Be Sure to Test Your Course in a Browser

If you are going to publish your course to SCORM or HTML to be viewed with a browser, then be aware of this warning.

Warning 38: While Lectora is WYSIWYG for the most part, it is not perfect due to differences in the way different browsers have implemented the HTML "standards." Just know that:

- Text blocks containing simple text, tables, or bulleted lines may get larger

- Pressing the Tab key may go through locations in a different sequence

- Transitions may look a bit different

For a more complete description of this topic, see the chapter on Lectora-HTML Differences later in this book.

Tip 147: Test Your Course in All Target Browsers

One browser may not be enough.

 **Warning 39:** Different Browsers: Be sure to test your courses out in all target browsers. Even IE8 and IE10 don't look the same. Here is an example.

IE 8

IE 10

| There are seven words on this line. This line has only five words. | There are seven words on this line. This line has only five words. |

B. Expediting the Review Process

Once you are satisfied with your course, you get several sets of eyes look over the course. Here are some tips to help you do that effectively along with several options on how to get the feedback from the reviewers and make the changes. They are divided into two groups:

- Tips on how to get them done right and on time
- Tips on how to quickly and accurately make the changes

Tips for Getting Reviews Done Right and on Time

These tips will help you get the kind of feedback you are looking for as well as *when* you are looking for it.

Tip 148: How to Prep the Reviewer

When you ask for their review, make it clear *what* you want them to focus on in their review. Provide a checklist of what you want the reviewer to look for when reviewing the course.

- Content completeness
- Level of detail to achieve objectives
- Flow of course
- Accuracy of questions and correct answers
- **SME reviewers**: Ask them to make sure the content is accurate and complete; in practice exercises and assessment questions, make sure that the answers flagged as the correct answers are in fact the correct ones and that the feedback is appropriate.
- **Corporate department reviewers**: ask to be sure that it complies with corporate guidelines (communication colors, language, legal guidelines, etc.).

- **Target audience reviewers**: ask for their overall impression and if practice exercises and assessment questions clear.

Tip 149: How to Get Your Reviews Back on Time

- Give them an estimate as to about how much time you think it will take.

- Indicate *when* you expect the review back or better yet, ask the SME in a phone call when they can get it to you.

- Get confirmation from the SME that they understand what is expected and be sure they *can* get it to you by your deadline. Remember they have their regular job to attend to as well as training.

- Then email him/her and copy the team or his/her manager.

Tip 150: Different Ways to Get Reviewer Feedback

There are several ways to have reviewers get their comments back to you. Pick the one that works the best for you in a given instance and reviewer type.

- Lectora's ReviewLink

- Export the course to MS Word

- Use the Translations tool

- MS Word table

- Old school hard copy

As with anything else, each has its own advantages and disadvantages.

Reviewer Feedback Using ReviewLink

Use ReviewLink. I wish I had used it more but my clients are kind of old school and still use methods we had before ReviewLink. The big advantage to ReviewLink is that they can see the course run in an LMS and make comments using areas around the page. However, new images cannot be provided by the reviewer if they see one that needs to be changed.

Reviewer Feedback Using Export to MS Word

You can export the course text to MS Word and they can make changes there.

First, where possible, arrange all the text blocks in the Title Explorer in the sequence that they appear on the page from top to bottom. This is the sequence that they will appear in the MS Word doc.

- Note, you may find many things duplicated on every page like a course title or page numbers. The solution is to first copy the AWT file. Open it and delete anything you don't want to show in the export. I usually just grab all the inherited items and delete them. Then go to step 2.

- In addition, if you have used objects like breadcrumbs or setting page names using actions, these will *not* appear in the Word doc. This is why I do not use these kinds of objects.

1. Then, File ribbon > Export > Word.

Now the reviewer can make changes to the MS Word doc. You can have them turn on Track changes in MS Word to find them easily. They can paste new images directly into the document.

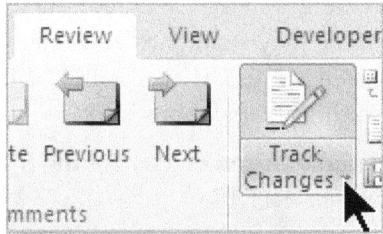

2. When you get it back from the reviewer, you go through looking for changes using the Next button on the Review ribbon in MS Word.

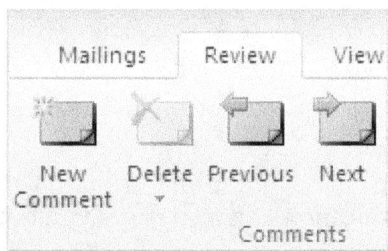

- If they forgot to turn on Track Changes, no worries. Just get the copy you sent them and compare it to what they sent to you using the Compare tool on the MS Word Review ribbon.

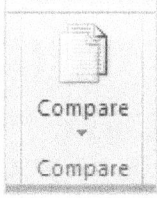

Note that you have to make all the text changes yourself in Lectora but at least you can copy and paste them.

Reviewer Feedback Using the Translations Tool

This is the only one of the options that automates the correction process to any degree. I.e., you don't have to copy and paste the corrections into Lectora.

You can export the course text using the Translation Tool in Lectora.

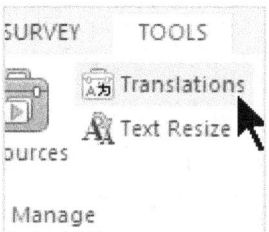

The reviewer makes all the changes in the exported text using WordPad. Then all you have to do is import the file they send back and make sure it imported correctly. No copying and pasting. IF YOU USE THIS METHOD, BE SURE TO READ THE CHAPTER ON Tips for Using the Translations Tool.

1. When you get it back from the reviewer, change the file name slightly, and put it in the folder with the original .RTF file.

2. Then open MS Word and on the Review ribbon, select Compare and compare the two documents.

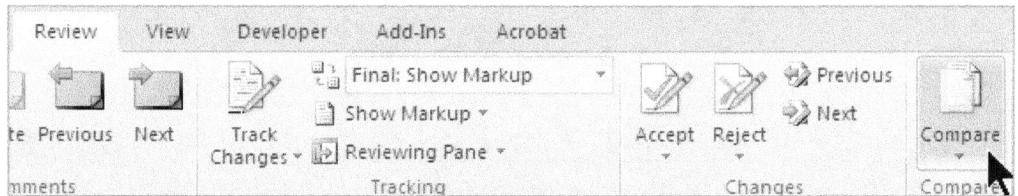

   This will give you an indication of which pages you need to review to be sure changes were made properly.

3. Next, copy your course AWT file in case something goes wrong.

4. Now Tools ribbon > Translation Tool > Import.

5. Finally, QA the changes by starting at the top in the MS Word document and compare and use the Next button on the Review ribbon to move to each change.

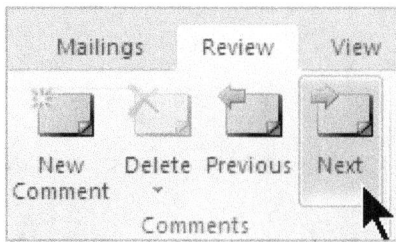

6. Check that page in Lectora to be sure it was made correctly and that the text block does not need adjusting.

Reviewer Feedback Using an MS Word Table

In the days before ReviewLink and Export to Word, I used this technique, which is a MS Word table with left column containing the page name of each page in the course. Here is how I created that table to send to the reviewer. All the reviewer had to do was find the page they wanted to correct and make an entry in the table.

1. On a blank page, add a Table of Contents as an Indented List.

2. Preview in browser and click on the TOC and grab all the text.

3. Then open Excel and paste. Each page name should go into the next row.

4. Grab the Excel table and paste into MS Word.

5. Add a column to the right and adjust the widths.

Old School

I use this when I am on site with clients and we are in the final review stage. I know there are only going to be a few corrections.

They simply print the page they want to make corrections on while reviewing. Then, they mark it up with a pen or pencil.

Very easy for just a few changes but you do have to type in any text changes yourself.

Tips for Making the Changes

Tip 151: How to Automate Updates from Reviewers

Here is a very quick way to make updates to text in your courses based on feedback from your SME. Have the reviewers make their changes to a translation file and pretty much all you have to do is import the file and all the changes are applied.

 **Warning 40:** Using the Translation Tool is a powerful and potentially dangerous technique. Be sure to read the chapter on Tips for Using the Translations Tool later in this book.

Create a file for the reviewer.

1. The sequence in which the text appears in the exported translation file is based on the sequence in which they appear in the Title Explorer (outline of the course usually on the left). So, first, arrange the text blocks in the Title Explorer in the sequence they appear on the page from top to bottom. Remember that the sequence in the Title Explorer affects layering so you may not be able to do this everywhere.

2. Next, Tools ribbon > Translation Tool > Export. This will create an RTF file.

3. Now, open that RTF file **using WordPad** and make sure the text blocks are in the right order. Do **not** use MS Word as it can embed unwanted characters.

4. Then send it to your reviewer instructing them to make changes using **WordPad**, **not** MS Word. MS Word puts all kinds of unsavory hidden characters in the text and you will suffer greatly if they use MS Word. You may have to help them find and use WordPad, which is usually included with the computer accessories. (No idea what to do on a Mac.)

Tip 152: Speeding Up Making Changes

When you go to make many manual changes to your course, the Title Explorer can present a challenge and slow you down. When you click on a page and start to make changes, the page expands in the Title Explorer. When it does, it pushes all the pages below it down. When you go to make edits on following pages, they may no longer be visible so you have to scroll down. In longer courses with lots of edits, you may have to scroll many many times.

Next time you have this situation, try this.

1. Right click on the first line in the Title Explorer and select Collapse All.

2. Close Lectora so that it remembers the collapsed Title Explorer.

3. Reopen the course and expand by clicking on the plus next to the level you collapsed.

4. Expand chapters and sections until you are almost at the page level.

5. Start at the *bottom* – the *last* page in the *last* chapter or section to make changes. The Title Explorer will expand but there is nothing below this page that matters so there is no problem.

This approach has two advantages:

• First, many more pages are still visible above it in the Title Explorer.

• As a side benefit, if your edits are based on page number and you add a page or delete an early page, then all the pages from there on are off from that point on. Very annoying. But, if you start at the bottom, this is not a problem as the earlier page numbers are still intact.

C. Publishing for an LMS

This section explains briefly how to set your course up to communicate with an LMS. It is a summary of what I have learned through trial and error as well as working with other Lectora developers and the Community forum. If you follow these instructions and they do not work, check with your LMS provider, as each LMS is different. If you want to try some of these with another LMS, you can use go to www.scorm.com and try it in their "cloud."

Tip 153: Set the Proper Title Options

In the Title Properties on the Content tab, select AICC/SCORM.

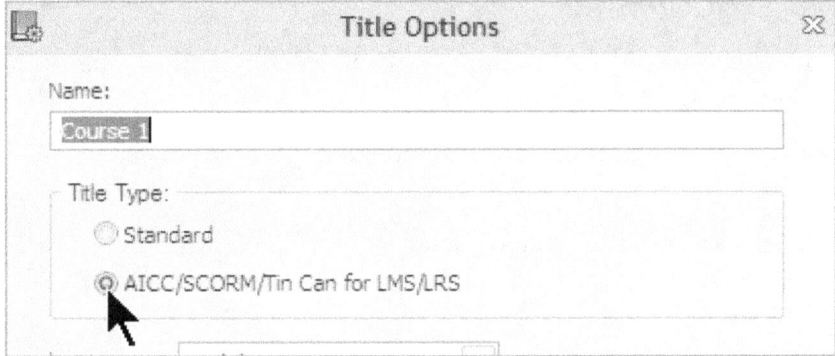

This will create a new level in your course called the Assignable Unit that you see in the Title Explorer.

On that same window, set the option to Retain completion status between sessions if you are using the status-tracking feature in Lectora 11.

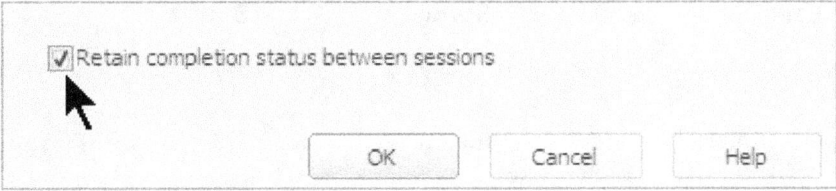

Tip 154: Set the AICC_Lesson_Status If No Test

Important Note: Settings in your LMS determine whether multiple attempts *override* previous values in the LMS, combined with them, or simply ignored.

You can use an OnShow action on a page (recommended) or an OnClick action on a button. If on a button, it **must** come before the Exit action. Keep in mind that sometimes learners will click the X in the upper right corner to close the window instead of clicking on a button to exit the course.

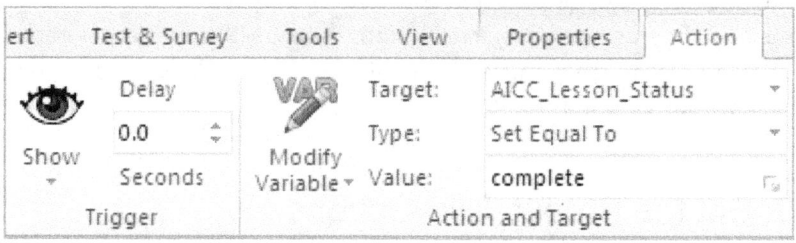

Published to SCORM 1.2

Here is what you can set the AICC_Lesson_Status to for SCORM 1.2 using the SCORM Cloud at SCORM.com.

AICC_Lesson_Status Value	LMS Completion Status	LMS Success Status
completed	complete	unknown
incomplete	incomplete	unknown
passed	complete	passed
failed	incomplete	failed

Published to SCORM 2004

Here is what you can set them to for SCORM 2004 using the SCORM Cloud at SCORM.com.

CMI_completion_Status Value	LMS Completion Status	LMS Success Status
completed	complete	???
incomplete	incomplete	???

Published to AICC

I do not have an AICC LMS to test on, but I know for completed at least one LMS requires a "c" instead of "completed." **If in doubt, check with your LMS support.**

Tip 155: Set the Passing Test Score in Two Places

It is just a good idea to set the passing score in two places: on the Test and on the assignable unit.

Click on the Test in the Title Explorer, then on the Results ribbon, check the Grade The Test box, and set your Passing Score.

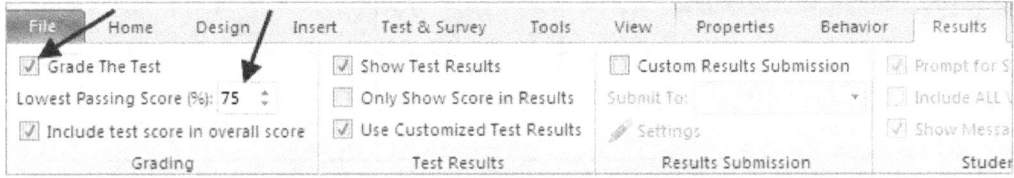

Just to be safe, you should also set the Mastery Score in the Assignable Unit Properties.

The Test score applies to the Test while the Mastery score applies to the *average* of *all* the Tests. So, if you have 2 Tests and the learner passes 1 and fails 1, their average score could still be above the Mastery score and they would pass the course.

Tip 156: How to Change the Button Text in the Standard Restart Window

The message in the restart window is one of the Publish Strings (File ribbon > Preferences).

"You have previously been in this lesson. Would you like to return to the last visited location in the lesson?"

The buttons that follow are OK and Cancel. Now OK is clear but cancel is a little confusing. You can experiment with No by finding the Cancel value in the published strings and changing it to No.

	Preferences		
General	String Set: Default Publish Strings	Add	Delete
Editors		Import	Export
CourseMill	Description:	Value:	
Lectora Express	The text that appears on the button that will close message/dialog boxes presented to the student.	OK	
ReviewLink			
Auto Update	The text that appears on the button that will cancel message/dialog boxes presented to the student.	Cancel	
Publish Strings			
Publish Messages	The text that appears on the button that	Print	

D. Coping with Storage Limits

This section covers LMS storage limits and gives you some ways to deal with them.

Warning 41: There is a **limit** as to how much data can be stored for each course and recalled the next time the student returns to the course.

> Non-LMS: 4k per course
>
> AICC: 4k per course
>
> SCORM 1.2: 4k per course
>
> SCORM 2004: 64k per course

You might ask how is the amount of data calculated? Here is a rough explanation, the best I have been able to determine. It is a fair approximation, and, as always, your mileage may vary.

- There is some standard overhead, not sure exactly what but I think something like 100 bytes.

- Each variable is stored as "variableName=value;"

  – For question variables, add the length of the question variable name, the length of the answer selected, and a couple more for separators (=;).

    Ex. "Question_0001=Coaching the individual;" takes 38 characters (bytes).

  – For your variables, it is the variable name, the length of whatever you store in the variable, and a couple more for separators.

- If you have used the Status Tracking introduced in Lectora 11 and retained it between sessions, then add 4 characters per page. Ex. a 100-page title will require a little over 400 characters.

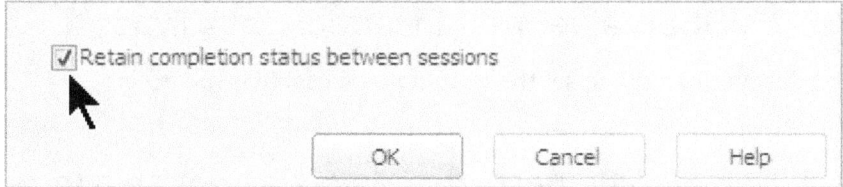

Here are some things you can do to keep your data requirements down.

Tip 157: Retain Only Necessary Variables

Review each retained variable and be sure that it really needs to be retained between sessions.

Tip 158: Keep Your Variable Names Short But Clear

Change the variable from Question_0001 to Q01 – a savings of 10 bytes per question – 100 questions ➜ 1000 bytes. Keep all your other variable names as short as possible but still clear enough so you remember what they are for.

Tip 159: Use Letters or Numbers Only in the Answer Choices

Then hide the answer text boxes and replace with a single text box containing the real answers. This way the answer text drops to only 1 character per question instead of 20-100. In our example above that took 38 characters we now have just 6 characters.

```
Q01=A;
```

Tip 160: Don't Use Questions That Require Text Input

Other than Fill-in-the-Blank questions, avoid Short Answer and Essay questions as they can chew up a lot of storage space in a hurry.

E. Common Error Messages or Problems

Tip 161: LMSSetValue Error: Data Model Element Type Mismatch

If you get this, your action to set the LMS status variable is incorrect. See the earlier sections in this paper about how to set the variables.

Tip 162: LMSSetValueError: Incorrect Data Type

If you get this, your action to set the LMS status variable is incorrect.

Tip 163: Some of the persistent data was not able to be stored

Possible known causes:

- You may have too much data being sent to the LMS. Compare how much data you are sending to the LMS (retained variables) to how much can be stored. See the Storage Limits section on the previous page.

- This is a message that the course produces when it passes a variable to the LMS' API adapter using an LMSSetValue() command and compares that with what it gets back from the API with an LMSGetValue() command. Somehow the data is being sent to the LMS and being changed before it comes back to be verified. If you have an On Show Go To or On Show Exit action on a page, give it a delay of .5to 1sec. This usually, but not always, fixes the problem.

Tip 164: Close Button Does Not Close Window Properly.

Make sure you have the publish option "The published course will be presented in a separate window than the LMS" checked. Close Button

In some cases the above does not work. If that happens to you, try this:

Add another action to the Exit button with:

```
On: Mouse Click
Action: Go To
Target: Web Address
Value: Javascript: top.window.close()
```

Thanks to Mallow76 of the UK

A recent tip from the Lectora forum by Tecocat was to "make sure that in your Publish options, you check the option that says 'Published Content will be Presented in a Separate window than the LMS.' This will enable you to use the Exit Title action in Lectora when publishing to SCORM."

Tip 165: Course Freezes as It Loads

Make sure you have the Also be sure to have the Use JavaScript Title Explorer option on the Options tab checked when you publish.

Tip 166: Unknown

From one of the users on the Lectora Community forum: "Lately we prepared a Test in one of our course and it worked fine in English but French users kept getting an error message. After discussion with our consultant developer about the fact that the problem resided with the French language I remembered having a language problem last year when we found that Lectora files with French accents would not be uploaded in our LMS. So working from this we discovered that although we can translate the values True or False into Vrai ou Faux, Lectora does not recognize it as a valid variable and keeps looking for it when we submit the Test. The work around was then to identify the type of question as a Multiple-choice option with Vrai ou Faux being the possible answers. It now works fine. "

Thanks to Pierrette Blanchette

F. Your Notes

When you find things that will help you when reviewing, publishing, and testing, make a note of them here.

4. Look Out for Lectora-HTML Differences

Like it or not, there are slight differences between the way things look and behave in Lectora (desktop version) and when viewed through a browser.

Lectora	HTML
Edit, Run, and Preview modes and published as a single file executable or CD	Preview in Browser and published to HTML, AICC, or SCORM

There are also differences *between browsers* including versions of IE. **Be sure you view your course using any potential browser.** With each new browser or release of Lectora, some of these will be fixed and some new ones may be introduced.

Let's look at how things *appear* differently and then how they *behave* differently.

A. Appearance

Slight differences are rampant. These are just the ones I have been able to collect. There may well be more.

Difference 1: Text Size

Blocks of text expand some, more if you use bullets. It also depends on the font. The line below each block of text is right at the bottom of the text when viewed in Lectora. As you can see, the Rendered as an Image preserves the Lectora look but it is just a little bit more to send up and down the communication lines plus it is not 508 compatible nor can someone select and copy the text.

	Rendered as an image
• bullet 9pt	• bullet 9pt
• bullet	• bullet
• bullet	• bullet
• bullet 10pt	• bullet 10pt
• bullet	• bullet
• bullet	• bullet
• bullet 11pt	• bullet 11pt
• bullet	• bullet
• bullet	• bullet

Difference 2: Bullets Size

Notice above that the bullets in the Lectora view above (right column) are bigger than the ones in the left column. While it says rendered as image, this is also the Lectora view.

Difference 3: Table Background Colors

When you use paragraph spacing above and below text to give a little margin above and below text (to keep it away from the edges of the table), it looks different. In Lectora the paragraph spacing is white, not the background color.

Lectora		HTML	
Physical Consequences	Elder abuse m sexually transr as the result o	**Physical Consequences**	Elder abuse m sexually transr as the result o
Emotional/ Psychological Consequences	Abused older ɛ psychological or fear. Victim: because of a ɑ	**Emotional/ Psychological Consequences**	Abused older ɛ psychological or fear. Victim: because of a ɑ
Social Consequences	Virtually all forr include increa: abuse and nec	**Social Consequences**	Virtually all forr include increaɛ abuse and nec

Difference 4: Text Blocks on Top of FLVs

In Lectora Edit mode, it looks transparent like the Browser below but when you run it, it is solid white.

Lectora	HTML
They appear as solid white	Appears transparent in HTML
Test text block	Test text block

Difference 5: SWF Transparency

Even if you have set the Parameter of wmode = transparent, the background will still appear not transparent (usually white) in Run or Preview mode. When viewed in a browser, the background is transparent when the wmode parameter is set.

Difference 6: Layering Objects on top of SWFs

If you layer an object on top of a SWF, it looks fine in Run and Preview modes but when viewed through a browser, the objects will appear *behind* the SWF unless you have set the Parameter wmode = transparent.

Difference 7: Popup Windows® Are Different

New window popups look just a bit different.

Lectora	HTML
Action = Display Message	Action = Display Message

Published with Use Lightbox *un*checked.

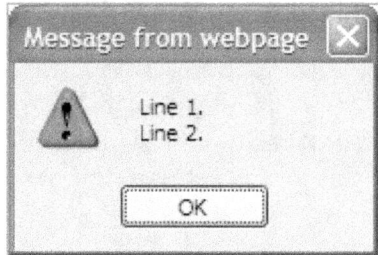

Published with Use Lightbox checked.

Action = Display Popup Page

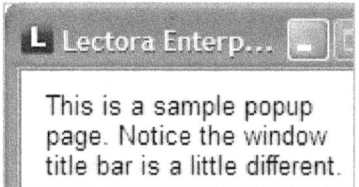

Action = Display Popup Page

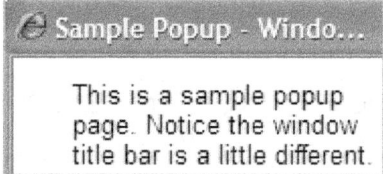

Action = GoTo Page in New Browser Window

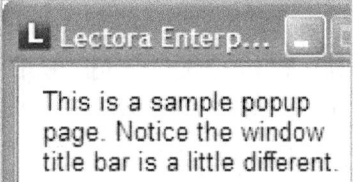

Action = GoTo Page in New Browser Window

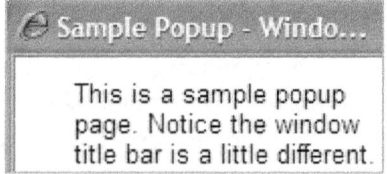

Action = GoTo Page in Lightbox Window
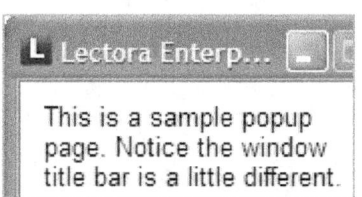
This is a sample popup page. Notice the window title bar is a little different.

Action = GoTo Page in Lightbox Window

Course 1

This is a sample popup page. Notice the window title bar is a little different.

Difference 8: Lightbox (Web 2.0) Popup Windows®

Lectora	HTML
Web 2.0 style popup Windows are not available. Popups appear as a new window.	Web 2.0 versions overlay the course with a transparent gray mask.

Difference 9: Text Wrapping Around Objects

Sometimes you get different wrapping depending on where the break is. See the images below.

Lectora	HTML
ı ipsum dolor sit amet, ctetuer adipiscing elit, sed diem nmy nibh euismod tincidunt ut	ipsum dolor sit amet, ctetuer adipiscing elit, sed ıonummy nibh euismod

Difference 10: RTF Text Files

The border is a bit different and even the margin on the left.

Lectora	HTML

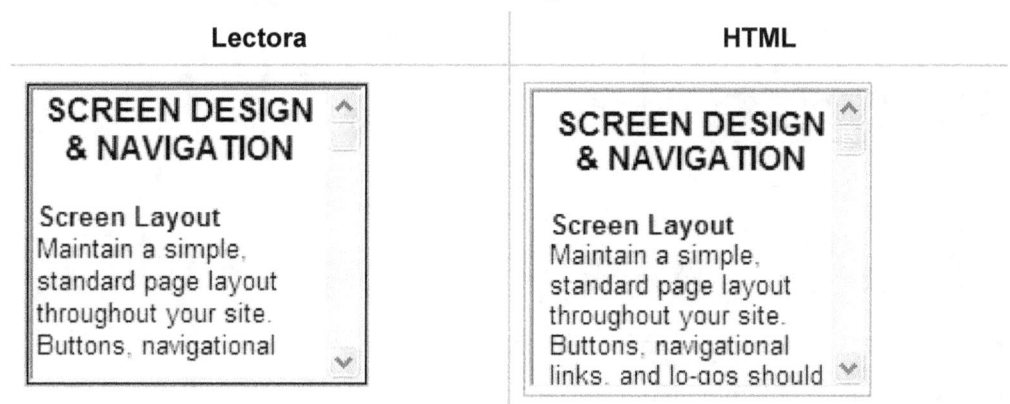

SCREEN DESIGN & NAVIGATION

Screen Layout
Maintain a simple, standard page layout throughout your site. Buttons, navigational

SCREEN DESIGN & NAVIGATION

Screen Layout
Maintain a simple, standard page layout throughout your site. Buttons, navigational links. and lo-gos should

Difference 11: Table of Contents Highlighting & Borders

Table of contents has different highlighting and different borders.

Tree View TOC

- Borders are different.
- HTML table is spread farther apart.
- Slightly less of the highlighted page name appears in browser.

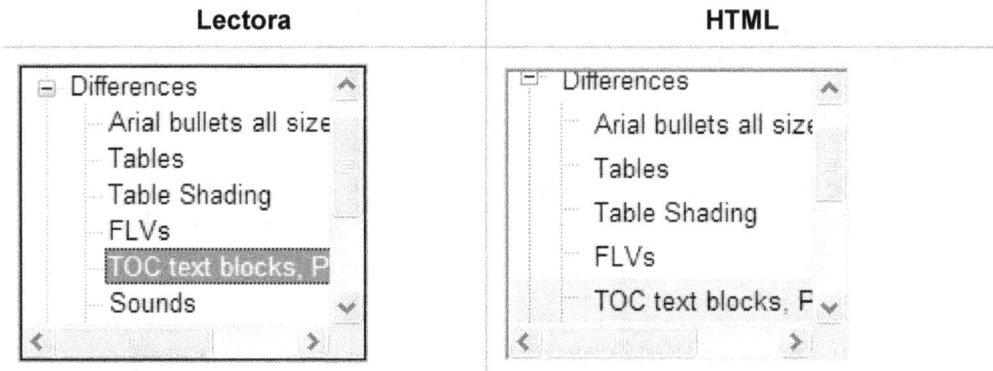

Indented List TOC

- Borders are different.
- Browser table is spread farther apart.
- Less of the highlighted page name appears.

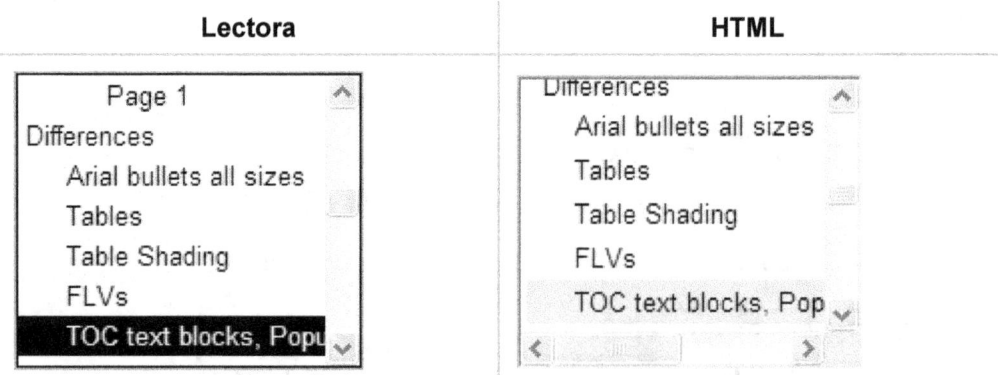

Dropdown List TOC

- Borders are different.
- Now the *Lectora* table is spread farther apart.
- More of the highlighted name appears in the *browser*

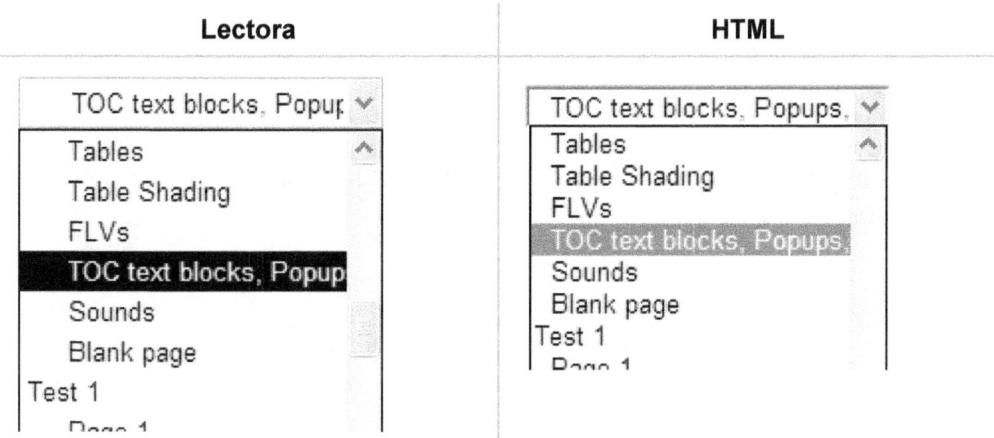

Lectora	HTML

Difference 12: ALT Tags

When you hover over a graphic:

Lectora	HTML
Alt tags (tool tips) do not show.	Will show unless you turn them off using the object properties or change the default publish option. Can be annoying or distracting.

Difference 13: Text Block Change Contents Action Using Multiple Lines

You can code \\r in text strings when using a Change Contents action to get the text to start on a new line. For example "line 1\\rline2 \\rline3" appears as shown below:

Lectora	HTML
line 1\\rline2 \\rline3	line
	line2
	line3

Difference 14: Form Elements

The check box, radio button, and entry field are slightly different if you do not use any of the alternates in Preferences.

Lectora	HTML
Radio button and check box are smaller and are black.	Check and radio button are larger and green.
Entry field has black border.	Entry field has blue border.
Bottom of text in drop-down list box is cut off.	

Difference 15: Lines in a Matching Question

If you have any kind of object (image, graphic, text box, …) in the white space between one column and the other, the blue matching lines appear differently.

Lectora	HTML
Lines are *behind* the object regardless of how you have it layered. Here the computer screen is layered at the Back.	Lines appear as expected based on layering.

Difference 16: Browser Scaling

It appears that if your learner has set the IE8 browser scale factor to something other than 100%, text boxes and graphics get scaled at slightly different amounts than the graphics. It does not seem to matter whether the graphics are BMP, JPG, GIF, or PNG. The workaround is to set your text boxes to be Rendered as an Image. This works pretty well except that the bullets will be different sizes. Sigh! I have not tested this with any other browsers.

- Test raw bullet
- Test bullet converted to image

Difference 17: Browser Differences

While this is not a Lectora-HTML difference, it relates to the above regarding appearance. When I viewed one of my courses in IE10 that looked fine in IE8, there were many differences. Some of the text blocks were cut off. Some graphics overlaying text blocks were no longer in alignment by a couple of px. Now that is not very bad, but still it looked unprofessional. When I made the corrections, I was concerned that it would no longer look right in IE8, but it looked just fine. No idea why.

Difference 18: Transitions

This is a Wipe Right transition. As it transitions in, in Lectora it looks fine but in HTML, the text is grainy and there is no border. After the transition is complete, it looks fine.

Lectora	HTML During Transition

When PNGs with partially transparent areas like this one with a shadow transition in, it looks fine in Lectora but in HTML, the shadow is black. After the transition is complete, it looks fine.

Difference 19: Table of Contents Looks Different

A client wanted a border around the word Contents and the actual dropdown TOC. When I lined it up in Lectora

Lectora

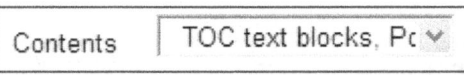

HTML

Difference 20: Debug Mode

Lectora

All the controls are at the bottom of the window.

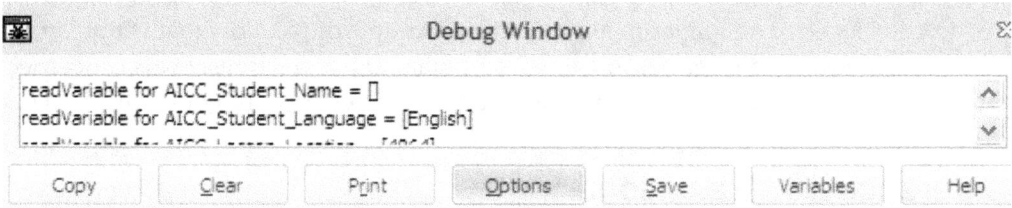

The Variables window shows all variables in the course.

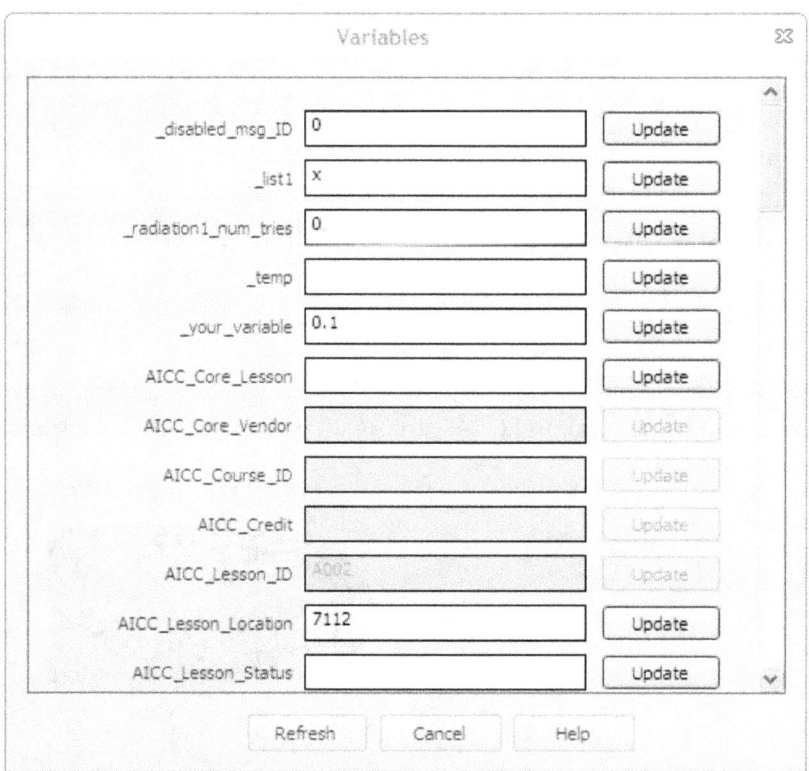

HTML

The limited controls are at the top of the window.

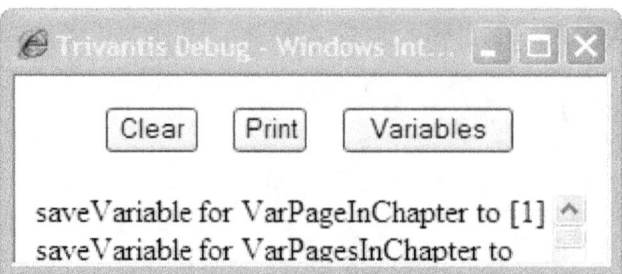

The Variables window shows only those variables available on that page.

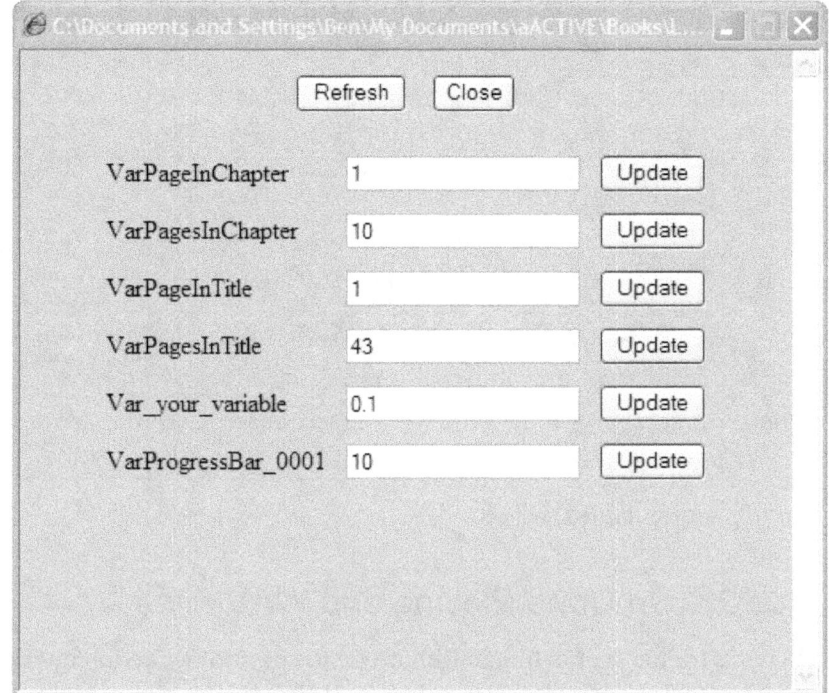

B. Execution/Operation/Behavior

Not only can your course look a little different but it also may work a little differently. Again, these are the ones I have collected. There are likely more.

Difference 21: Publish Errors Do Not Appear

This is one of the most important differences. If you have errors and just click Run, Preview, or Preview in Browser mode, you will not see them and your actions may not run correctly. So, whenever you have actions that are not working right in Run or Preview mode, Publish to see the errors. Preview in Browser may in fact show a distorted screen.

Difference 22: Test Results Page

Tests work fine in Run mode with Next Page specified on Passed tab and no following page in the course but not in HTML. Sometimes the Test Results page will not show up. Sometimes it won't post properly to the LMS. You have to add a page after the Test Chapter.

Replace

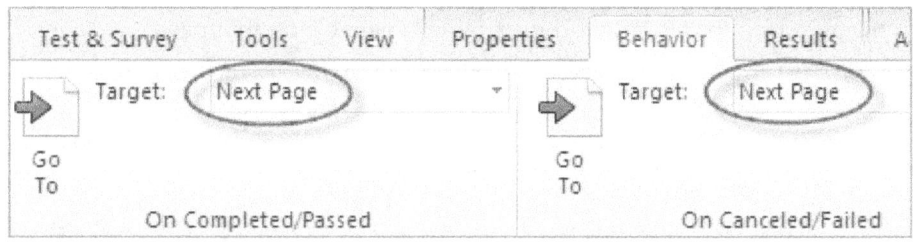

with

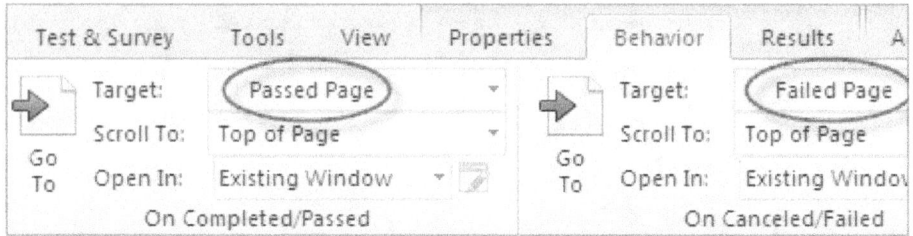

which point to pages outside the Test.

Difference 23: On Done Playing and WAV Files

On Done Playing trigger works fine in Run mode to cue another action but not in HTML. You have to convert the files to MP3s or FLVs which is a publish option.

Difference 24: JavaScript in HTML Objects

JavaScript and JQuery code does not run unless viewed through a browser.

Difference 25: HTML

The HTML and CSS does not work unless viewed through a browser.

Difference 26: Keyboard Shortcuts

Lectora	HTML
Ctrl-P does *not* print the page.	Ctrl-P prints the page.
Backspace does not do anything.	Backspace takes you to the previous page.

Difference 27: Opening a PDF

When you use the Open Attachment action to open a PDF, they look slightly different. A lot depends on your browser and the type of PDF reader you have.

Lectora	HTML
Opens a window using the PDF reader you have installed. The controls across the top are for the reader.	Opens the PDF in a browser window and depending on your software, it will usually look different than just the plain PDF reader.

Difference 28: Debug Mode

Lectora

Shows all the actions from all the pages viewed so far.

You can make the debug window taller but not wider or narrower.

Has buttons for Copy, Options, Save, and Help that are not in the HTML window. (The Options for HTML are set when it is published.)

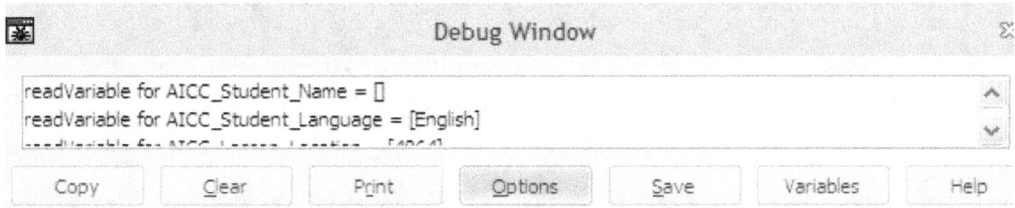

HTML

Only shows the actions for the currently showing page so you cannot see the actions that happened as you left the last page before coming to the current one. One work-around is to put a Display Message on the previous page that runs when the page hides.

You can make the debug window taller and wider or narrower.

It has fewer controls.

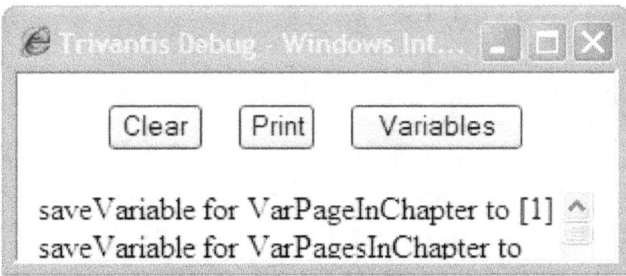

The debug options are set by clicking Options when publishing.

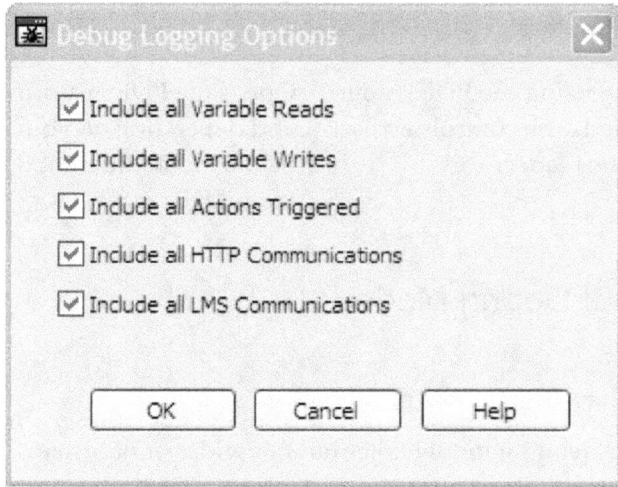

Difference 29: Send Mail Action

Lectora	HTML
First opens a browser window with nothing in it and *then* opens up an email using the default email client on the user's computer.	Simply opens up an email using the default email client on the user's computer.

Difference 30: Submitting Forms & Data to a Database

When you submit forms or data to a database or a server using server-side scripts, it appears that Run mode and .exe versions have problems.

Difference 31: Flash Commands

One user has reported that commands in Flash like the below do not work in Run mode, just when published to HTML, etc.

Set a Lectora variable: ExternalInterface.call("Varvariablename.set('value')");

Get a Lectora variable value: ExternalInter-face.call("Varvariablename.getValue()");

Run a Lectora Action Group: ExternalInterace.call("runGroup_objectname()");

Hide an object: ExternalInterface.call("objectname.actionHide()");

Show an object: ExternalInterface.call("objectname.actionShow()");

Next Page: ExternalInterface.call("trivNextPage()");

Previous Page: ExternalInterface.call("trivPrevPage()");

Difference 32: Audio Controller Volume

Lectora	HTML
Resets to max volume on each page.	Once set on one page, it is the same on all the other pages.

And there are probably more that I haven't caught. Just be sure to test your course in the target publishing mode on all target browsers.

C. Your Notes

When you find more differences, make a note of them here.

5. Tips for Using the Translations Tool

The Translations tool was designed to aid in translating your course from one language to another. It does not actually do the translation but rather creates a file with all the text that needs to be translated. It is a powerful tool to have in your tool kit. However, there are a couple of important things you should know.

- It works pretty well as long as you follow the tips in this chapter. Failure to do so can result in some serious problems with your course.

- It can be used for things other than changing languages like mass changes in large courses or automating corrections from reviewers.

The tips in this chapter are organized around the process of using the tool.

Warning 42: Proceed with caution: While the translation tool is very useful, I need to start out with a warning before you get burned. Sometimes the importing of the translation file will *mess up buttons, especially multi-line ones as well as numbered lists.* Initial testing with Lectora 11.3.1 seems to show that some of these problems have been solved. However, there *may* be issues with buttons and lists coming from previous versions of Lectora.

In this example, the button looks fine but it did change the name in the Title Explorer. Not a big deal, but still annoying.

Before Translation	**After Translation**

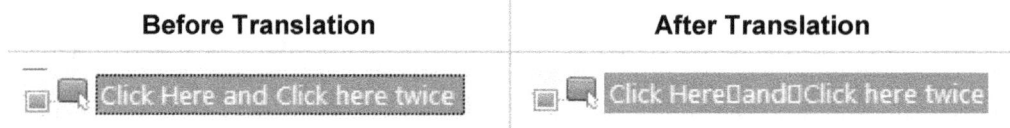

A. Do These Things *During* Development to Prepare for Translation

While developing the original course, heed these warnings. Doing so will make your life much easier later when you use the translation tool.

Warning 43: Don't use the ability to set the contents of a text box by using an action because translation export does not export this text.

Warning 44: Do not click on a text box and center it or apply any kind of formatting to it (indents, bullets, etc.). Instead, click inside the text box, select the desired text, and format as desired. Formatting applied to the box as a whole is sometimes lost when the text is imported.

Warning 45: Make text blocks a little higher than needed. Even though there is a box, you can check to expand them, it is better to do this during design and allow for the extra space needed.

Warning 46: Verdana font usually does not expand text blocks. Arial frequently expands over-running the text blocks.

Warning 47: Avoid white text. You cannot see white text on a white background and it will make it hard for the translator. When you export, your white text is on a white RTF file. There is no way to change the background color in WordPad, your translating tool. While you can in MS Word, you are very likely to import with a mess because MS Word embeds hidden characters that show up, *not* in Lectora, but when it is published to HTML.

Warning 48: Avoid putting images in text boxes. They sometimes end up at the beginning of the box instead of where they were in the middle.

Warning 49: Avoid tables if you can help it. You would be amazed how much you depend on words being the right size.

Warning 50: Avoid Flash objects that contain text, as there is no easy way to translate them.

Warning 51: Avoid buttons created with Title Wizards. Buttons created with the Button Wizard are translated. Buttons included with the Title Wizards are **not**.

B. Do This *Before* You Send the Translation File Out

Warning 52: There are some circumstances where the Translation Tool may not work well for your course. As yet, I have not been able to identify just what those circumstances are but they do occur. Perform this quick check before you get too far down the road and save yourself some grief.

1. Copy the AWT file just in case things go haywire.
2. Export the translation file and immediately import it.

3. Now, check:
   - all your multi-line buttons. Look at them in the layout pane on the right and check their names in the left pane
   - your numbered lists to see if they are still correct
   - for any unusual characters in text blocks
4. Now publish to HTML and check again. THIS IS CRITICAL!

If everything looks fine, then send the translation file to your translator or reviewer.

C. Do These Things *During* Translation

You should probably summarize these things in a set of instructions to your translator.

Tip 167: How to Translate Hyperlinks

Warning 53: Be careful when translating hyperlinks or you can mess up the URL.

Sometimes you will need to do something special to translate links and retain the URL. Suppose you had "Click here for more info" to translate as a link.

1. Click after the first letter and delete all but the last letter. So here, "Click here for more info" becomes "Co".

2. Click after the "C" and enter the translated text.

3. Delete the "C" and the "o".

Tip 168: Beware That the Translator May Have Used the Wrong Tool

Warning 54: MS Word tends to introduce hidden characters that don't show up until published and viewed with a browser.

Use something WordPad or possibly DreamWeaver to translate. These tools do not introduce unnecessary characters. WordPad is free and native to most Windows® systems.

When you get the translated file back from the translator, open it in WordPad, and look it over. If you find paragraphs with 1), 2), etc. in front of them, change to bullets or know you will have to fix in Lectora. It is easier to change them here in WordPad.

D. Do This *When* You Import

Tip 169: How to Avoid a Translation Import Crisis

Warning 55: Know that no matter how much you check your translation file, things can still go wrong.

Copy your AWT file – the Lectora source file – *before* you import the translation file. Do this in the Windows® File Explorer. Just copy and paste right where it is. If something goes wrong, you can recover easily by deleting the trashed file and renaming the copy to the original name.

Tip 170: One Way to Reduce Your Workload

Select the Expand text blocks option when you start the import. While this will help reduce your work a bit, you still need to check every page *after* you have published to be sure the text blocks are big enough.

E. Do These Things *After* You Import

Tip 171: Check the Translated File Size

Warning 56: Once in a great while the AWT file will get 10-15 times bigger! Immediately check the size of the new AWT file. I had one go from 2MB to 30MB. If yours expanded by several meg, try this. Many people have had success with it.

1. Back up one step and open the translated RTF file in WordPad.
2. Click in front of the first character and then scroll down to the last line, hold the shift key down and click just before the last character.
3. Copy.
4. Create a **new** RTF document and paste.
5. Retype the last character.
6. Save.
7. Import this file into Lectora as the translated file.

No, I don't know why this works but it does. Your new file size will be fairly close to the old one.

Tip 172: Look for Things That May Have Changed

Warning 57: Some things can get changed during import. Here is a list of the things to look for.

-   Start and the last page and work up so you don't have to keep scrolling down to get more pages. The expanded pages will scroll off the bottom of the left pane.
-   Check button sizes. If the translated text was bigger than the previous text, it may need to be opened and have its size adjusted.
-   Check Fill-in-the-blank questions again to be sure the correct answer is recognized and for **length**.
-   If you had objects in text boxes, they end up at the front of the box instead of where they were. Find those boxes and repair.
-   Check **bullets** - sometimes they seem to get dropped or are too small.
-   Check centering of text. Sometimes this ends up left justified. The cause seems to be applying centering to the text block instead of to the paragraphs within the text block.

- Look for text built with actions such as page numbering that still needs to be translated.

- If you have some all upper case phrases that did not get translated to all upper case, you can copy the text to MS Word and use the Change Case tool under the Format ribbon, then copy and paste unformatted into Lectora.

- Publish to HTML and review. Many times things look fine in Lectora but not when published, especially the lines beginning with 0), 1), etc. mentioned above.

- Remember that you can import the same text more than once. If you find changes are easier to make in the RTF file, go back, make them, and then re-import.

- If you find that some text blocks are too big, here are a few options:
  - Drop the font size down one pixel.
  - Open Properties of the text box and select the Convert To Image property.

F. Your Notes

When you find your own tips for translating, make a note of them here.

Appendix 1: Summary
of All Warnings

Introduction—1

1. General Tips for Faster Development—5

A. Get the Right Hardware and Software Configuration—6

Warning 1: Using any Display setting in Windows® other than 100% can result in faulty page layout.—8

Warning 2: Unlike MS Word where both copies reflect changes made in either one, **Lectora copies are independent**. If you make changes to the first and save and close it then make changes to the second and save it, the changes to the first are GONE!—9

B. Make Life Easier with These Across-the-Board Lectora Tips—9

Warning 3: You can accidently open the wrong course if you launch Lectora first.—11

Warning 4: Be absolutely sure you know what you are doing and which folder you are in when using Save As.—11

Warning 5: You can have problems if you open a course that is somewhere other than on your C drive. Not always, but when it does happen, the errors and problems do not indicate that the problem is related to where the course is stored.—12

C. Use the Title Explorer like an Expert—14

D. Layout like a Pro—18

Warning 6: It is *not* enough just to have guides. You also need to have turned on Snap to Guides.—22

Warning 7: Sometimes but not always, when you change the size of an image, it may look fine in Lectora but *distort when published and viewed using a browser*. So, if you do change its size, be sure to Preview in Browser to be sure.—26

Warning 8: When replacing graphics, all the graphics should be the *same size* or you will get some distortion. If your graphics are different sizes

129

and you want to use this technique, then put the smaller ones on a white background the same size as the largest one and create a new graphic.—28

Warning 9: If you do text, know that the spell checker does not check the text as of Lectora 11.—28

E. Making Your Own Reusable Learning Objects—28

Warning 10: Do not use any of the prohibited characters for a Windows® file name (/*?:<>|.) used in the name of the first object.—32

Warning 11: The worst one and most common is using a colon (:). You get NO WARNING that it could not save it. It acts like it saved it. Therefore, best practice here is to check right after you save one and be sure it is there. If not, check the name.—33

Warning 12: Variable Names: While you can save questions and form objects, know that when they are reused later they will create a *new variable name if the one in the library object is already in use.* There is a workaround for this discussed later. Examples:—33

Warning 13: Lectora keeps its library objects where they may not be backed up.—33

Warning 14: Actions Referencing Objects: You may have actions in your Library object that reference objects not in the object like popup pages, hiding the Next button, or running an action group at the title level. When you insert the Library object the next time, all these references are broken. Your best alternative here is to put your RLO in the course itself in the Development chapter (discussed later).—34

F. Your Notes—34

2. Power Tips for Specific Objects—35

A. Text Tips—35

Warning 15: However, unlike MS Word, the styles are *not* coded below the surface with hidden codes. What that means is that if you have two styles that are the same but different names and you change one, it will change all the text using either text style.—37

Warning 16: Further, unlike MS Word, it will not change text with any formatting modification like bold, italics, or a different color.—37

Warning 17: If you don't know already, it is generally a **very bad idea** to copy and simply paste text from another application directly into Lectora. When you use a simple copy and paste of text from another application, you run the risk of copying in all kinds of hidden formatting. This hidden formatting does not always work well in Lectora. Or, even worse, when you viewed from a browser lots of things look different – you have new bullets where there are none in Lectora, spacing is all off, etc.—41

Warning 18: If you use special fonts that are not generally available, when your course is viewed by someone who does not have those fonts, the browser will substitute another similar font. The spacing may not be what you expect.—42

Warning 19: The Translation Tool is a powerful and potentially dangerous tool. Be sure to read the chapter on Tips for Using the Translations Tool later in this book.—45

Warning 20: Sometimes those graphics inside text blocks suddenly all end up at the beginning of the block. This seems to happen only on rare occasions and I think if you import from a translation file.—46

Warning 21: Lectora does *not* flag misspelled words *unless* your cursor is actually inside the text block.—46

Warning 22: Lectora does *not* flag misspelled words when the text is changed using a Change Contents action.—46

B. Working with Bullets and Tables—48

C. Working with Graphics—49

Warning 23: Sometimes graphics that use the CMYK (Cyan, Magenta, Yellow, blacK) color scheme instead of RBG (Red, Blue, Green) will not display correctly in a browser. I have not yet been able to narrow down the exact conditions but it seems to happen rarely with courses viewed from an LMS rather than simply viewed from the desktop.—50

Warning 24: If you resize an image, it may look fine in Lectora but when published to HTML it may look grainy or pixelated. It is better to resize images in the source tool (PhotoShop, PowerPoint®, etc.).—52

Warning 25: If you continually copy and paste directly from a drawing tool, Lectora creates a *new* image each time you paste. For example, if you used the same PowerPoint® diagram on three different pages, copying each time from PowerPoint® and just pasting into Lectora, Lectora now has three *different* images in the images folder. If you decide to change the diagram, you have to go to all three places to change it.—53

Warning 26: Your images folder will sometimes have graphics left over from past work. Lectora 11 at least has no easy way of deleting unused images from the images folder. Same with video and audio file files.—54

D. Buttons and Menus—56

Warning 27: Be aware that Lectora will *not* change the button file name. Say the first one was Next. Its file name in Windows® is next.gif. You copy it in Lectora and change the text to Back. But the file name is next001.gif, *not* back.gif.—56

E. Tips when Using Groups—60

Warning 28: Oh, do not use a colon (Ex. actions:) because if you ever try to save it as a Lectora Library object, it will not save but Lectora will *not* warn you! It simply does not save it. Bummer.—62

F. Tips for Actions and Variables—62

Warning 29: Don't name your Lectora pages using a period. A community forum member named one "offensive lang." and it messed up the coding later causing the LMS unable to display that page. Why, you ask? It ended up causing two periods side by side (..) in the source coding.—64

Warning 30: While it is a nice idea, retaining variable values between sessions can cause problems. Most LMSs have a limit of 4K. If you start retaining all your variables, you could exceed that limit and cause unpredictable behavior when the course is launched the second time. See Coping with Storage Limits on page 102.—68

G. Popup Window Tips—68

H. Power Tips for Tests and Questions—69

Warning 31: If you have no pages after your Test (no popup chapter, no development chapter, no nothing), then scored Tests will work in Run mode but *not* when published to HTML.—71

Warning 32: One caution is that if you copy the questions into another part of the title or another title, the question numbers are likely to change but the names of the questions in the Title Explorer will not. You will have to manually go in and change those names yourself.—73

Warning 33: Using partial credit (checking the Grade each choice box) to allow the student to get some credit can lead to very confusing scoring.—76

I. Tips for Miscellaneous Objects—81

J. Your Notes—83

3. Reviewing, Publishing, and Testing Tips—85

A. Publishing & Testing Considerations—85

Warning 34: You may have errors that do *not* show when you try your course in Run or Preview modes. These errors *only* show when you Publish your course.—86

Warning 35: I have seen the publish option "Publish Only Updated Pages/Resources" *not* publish pages where only the actions had been changed.—88

Warning 36: As I said before, the Translation Tool is a powerful and potentially dangerous technique. Be sure to read the chapter on Tips for Using the Translations Tool later in this book to avoid all the pitfalls.—89

Warning 37: Things can look a lot different to the learner depending on the browser zoom setting. Don't take chances. View your course with different zoom settings.—92

Warning 38: While Lectora is WYSIWYG for the most part, it is not perfect due to differences in the way different browsers have implemented the HTML "standards." Just know that:—92

Warning 39: Different Browsers: Be sure to test your courses out in all target browsers. Even IE8 and IE10 don't look the same. Here is an example.—93

B. Expediting the Review Process—93

Warning 40: Using the Translation Tool is a powerful and potentially dangerous technique. Be sure to read the chapter on Tips for Using the Translations Tool later in this book.—97

C. Publishing for an LMS—99

D. Coping with Storage Limits—102

Warning 41: There is a **limit** as to how much data can be stored for each course and recalled the next time the student returns to the course.—102

E. Common Error Messages or Problems—103

F. Your Notes—105

4. Look Out for Lectora-HTML Differences—107

A. Appearance—108

B. Execution/Operation/Behavior—117

C. Your Notes—122

5. Tips for Using the Translations Tool—123

Warning 42: Proceed with caution: While the translation tool is very useful, I need to start out with a warning before you get burned. Sometimes the importing of the translation file will *mess up buttons, especially multi-line ones as well as numbered lists*. Initial testing with Lectora 11.3.1 seems to show that some of these problems have been solved. However, there *may* be issues with buttons and lists coming from previous versions of Lectora.—123

A. Do These Things *During* Development to Prepare for Translation—124

Warning 43: Don't use the ability to set the contents of a text box by using an action because translation export does not export this text.—124

Warning 44: Do not click on a text box and center it or apply any kind of formatting to it (indents, bullets, etc.). Instead, click inside the text box, select the desired text, and format as desired. Formatting applied to the box as a whole is sometimes lost when the text is imported.—124

Warning 45: Make text blocks a little higher than needed. Even though there is a box, you can check to expand them, it is better to do this during design and allow for the extra space needed.—124

Warning 46: Verdana font usually does not expand text blocks. Arial frequently expands over-running the text blocks.—124

Warning 47: Avoid white text. You cannot see white text on a white background and it will make it hard for the translator. When you export, your white text is on a white RTF file. There is no way to change the background color in WordPad, your translating tool. While you can in MS Word, you are very likely to import with a mess because MS Word embeds hidden characters that show up, *not* in Lectora, but when it is published to HTML.—124

Warning 48: Avoid putting images in text boxes. They sometimes end up at the beginning of the box instead of where they were in the middle.—124

Warning 49: Avoid tables if you can help it. You would be amazed how much you depend on words being the right size.—124

Warning 50: Avoid Flash objects that contain text, as there is no easy way to translate them.—124

Warning 51: Avoid buttons created with Title Wizards. Buttons created with the Button Wizard are translated. Buttons included with the Title Wizards are **not**.—124

B. Do This *Before* You Send the Translation File Out—125

Warning 52: There are some circumstances where the Translation Tool may not work well for your course. As yet, I have not been able to identify just what those circumstances are but they do occur. Perform this quick check before you get too far down the road and save yourself some grief.—125

C. Do These Things *During* Translation—125

Warning 53: Be careful when translating hyperlinks or you can mess up the URL.—125

Warning 54: MS Word tends to introduce hidden characters that don't show up until published and viewed with a browser.—126

D. Do This *When* You Import—126

Warning 55: Know that no matter how much you check your translation file, things can still go wrong.—126

E. Do These Things *After* You Import—127

Warning 56: Once in a great while the AWT file will get 10-15 times bigger! Immediately check the size of the new AWT file. I had one go from 2MB to 30MB. If yours expanded by several meg, try this. Many people have had success with it.—127

Warning 57: Some things can get changed during import. Here is a list of the things to look for.—127

F. Your Notes—128

Index